Keto Diet for S

Evelyn Hartley

Table of contents

Introduction

Foreword

Welcome to **"Keto Diet for Seniors"**, a comprehensive guide designed to empower you with the knowledge and tools needed to adopt a ketogenic lifestyle that aligns with the unique needs of aging adults. This book is not just a collection of recipes; it is a tailored blueprint that includes detailed dietary guidance, dual-measurement recipes, meticulous meal planners, and carefully curated exercise strategies to foster healthy living.

Why a keto book specifically for seniors? As we age, our bodies undergo various changes that can affect our nutritional needs, physical capabilities, and health outcomes. The ketogenic diet, known for its effectiveness in managing weight, enhancing cognitive function, and stabilizing energy levels, can benefit seniors. However, adopting such a diet can seem daunting without the proper guidance.

This book is crafted to make the ketogenic diet approachable and enjoyable for seniors, whether they're beginners or well-acquainted with keto principles. We've translated complex nutritional science into easy-to-understand language and provided practical tools to help them succeed. Each recipe includes measurements in both ounces and grams, catering to diverse cooking preferences and making the process as straightforward as possible.

Moreover, physical health extends beyond diet. Recognizing this, we have included a comprehensive exercise guide tailored to seniors. These exercise plans complement the ketogenic diet and focus on enhancing balance and stability, which are crucial for preventing falls and maintaining independence.

As you embark on this journey, remember that this book is more than just a manual; it is a companion in your quest for a healthier, more vibrant life. We understand the challenges and concerns of age and have addressed these with thoughtful content that resonates with and supports your lifestyle.

Thank you for choosing this path with us. We are excited to be a part of your journey to health and vitality, providing support every step of the way. Whether you want to revitalize your diet, incorporate new physical activities, or gain more energy to enjoy your golden years, **"Keto Diet for Seniors"** guides you through each moment with confidence and joy.

Let's begin this transformative journey together.

Sincerely,

Evelyn Hartley

Overview of the Ketogenic Lifestyle for Seniors

The ketogenic lifestyle offers a transformative approach to health and wellness, especially for seniors seeking to enhance their quality of life. This lifestyle is centered around a diet high in fats, moderate in proteins, and very low in carbohydrates, which prompts the body to enter a state known as ketosis. In ketosis, the body becomes incredibly efficient at burning fat for energy, leading to various health benefits that are particularly advantageous for older adults.

Key Benefits of the Ketogenic Diet for Seniors

1. **Improved Cognitive Function**: Maintaining cognitive health becomes crucial as we age. The ketogenic diet has been shown to offer neuroprotective benefits, potentially helping preserve memory and cognitive function by providing the brain with ketones as a potent energy source.

2. **Enhanced Energy and Vitality**: Many seniors experience fluctuations in energy levels, often due to unstable blood sugar levels. Keto helps stabilize these levels, providing a more consistent energy source that can enhance overall vitality and stamina.

3. **Weight Management**: Managing weight can become more challenging with age due to a natural decline in metabolic rate. The ketogenic diet aids in weight loss by reducing appetite and increasing satiety through high-fat and protein-rich meals.

4. **Reduced Inflammation**: Chronic inflammation is common in older adults and can contribute to various diseases. The ketogenic diet has anti-inflammatory properties, which can help reduce overall inflammation and pain, leading to improved mobility and quality of life.

5. **Management of Diabetes**: Type 2 diabetes is prevalent among seniors. The ketogenic diet, by lowering carbohydrate intake, can help control blood sugar levels and improve insulin sensitivity.

Adapting Keto to Senior Lifestyles

Adopting any new diet can be challenging, and for seniors, specific considerations must be made to ensure the transition is safe and effective. Tailoring the ketogenic diet to accommodate dietary restrictions, potential medication interactions, and individual nutritional needs is crucial.

Safety Measures and Nutritional Considerations

- **Consultation with Healthcare Providers**: Before starting any new diet, particularly for those with pre-existing health conditions, consulting with a healthcare provider is essential. They can offer guidance tailored to your health profile.

- **Adequate Nutrient Intake**: It is vital to ensure a balanced intake of nutrients. Seniors should incorporate various keto-friendly foods to meet their micronutrient and fiber needs.

- **Hydration and Electrolyte Balance**: Seniors are more susceptible to dehydration and shifts in electrolyte balance. It's essential to drink plenty of fluids and consider supplementing with electrolytes if recommended by a healthcare provider.

- **Gradual Transition**: Easing into the ketogenic diet can help mitigate initial side effects, such as the keto flu, and allow the body time to adjust to new energy sources.

The ketogenic lifestyle can be a powerful tool for seniors looking to regain control over their health and well-being. Careful planning, consultation, and adaptation can significantly improve energy levels, cognitive function, and overall vitality, making the golden years truly golden. Embracing this lifestyle change under the guidance of this book will provide seniors with the knowledge and resources needed to successfully integrate the ketogenic diet into their daily lives, ensuring it is a rewarding and sustainable journey.

Benefits of Choosing This Book

"Keto Diet for Seniors" is designed to be more than just a diet book; it's a comprehensive guide explicitly tailored to the needs and challenges faced by seniors interested in adopting a ketogenic lifestyle. Here are several reasons why choosing this book will be particularly beneficial for seniors looking to enhance their health and vitality:

1. Tailored Content for Seniors

Understanding that seniors have specific dietary and physical requirements, this book offers customized advice that addresses the unique health considerations of aging. From managing chronic conditions to ensuring adequate nutrient intake, the guidance provided is specifically designed to support the health and well-being of older adults.

2. Dual Measurement Recipes

Recognizing that readers come from diverse backgrounds with different preferences for recipe measurements, every recipe in this book includes ingredients listed in ounces and grams. This thoughtful feature ensures ease of use and accessibility, regardless of your preferred measurement system.

3. Comprehensive Meal Plans and Exercise Strategies

The book includes detailed 28-day meal plans and exercise strategies tailored to senior capabilities and needs. These plans complement the ketogenic diet, helping you achieve optimal results while maintaining safety and enhancing your overall physical fitness.

4. Practical and Actionable Advice

Every chapter provides practical tips that you can immediately implement. Whether it's advice on how to start the keto diet, suggestions for exercises that improve balance and reduce fall risk, or strategies to manage the side effects of dietary changes, the book offers actionable steps that make transitioning to a keto lifestyle manageable and sustainable.

5. Educational Insights into Ketogenic Science

We break down the science behind the ketogenic diet in a way that is easy to understand, dispelling myths and providing clear explanations of how ketosis works, especially in older adults. This foundational knowledge empowers you to make informed decisions about your health.

6. Inspirational Success Stories

The book includes real-life success stories from seniors who have thrived on the ketogenic diet to motivate and inspire. These stories provide inspiration and practical insights into the challenges and triumphs of adopting keto later in life.

7. Resource for Continuous Support

This book is an ongoing resource, with tips for setting up a support network, resources for further reading, and guidance on adjusting your diet as your needs change. This makes it a valuable tool for long-term lifestyle adaptation.

8. Expertly Crafted by a Trusted Author

Written by Evelyn Hartley, an author committed to promoting senior health and wellness, this book offers trustworthy and researched-backed content designed to provide the highest information standard in senior nutrition and fitness.

Choosing **"Keto Diet for Seniors"** means selecting a resource that respects your journey toward a healthier lifestyle, supports your individual needs, and guides you every step in your transition to a ketogenic lifestyle. It's the ideal companion for any senior eager to explore the benefits of keto, with the assurance of having a knowledgeable guide by their side.

Chapter 1: The basics of aging and a ketogenic diet

Understanding Physical Changes in Seniors

As we age, our bodies undergo a series of natural physical changes that can affect our health, lifestyle, and dietary needs. Recognizing and understanding these changes is crucial for seniors who wish to adopt a ketogenic diet effectively and safely. This subchapter aims to provide a clear overview of the common physical transformations associated with aging and how they can impact nutritional requirements and diet choices.

1. Decreased Metabolic Rate

One of the most significant changes as we age is the slowing down the metabolic rate. This decrease means seniors burn fewer calories while at rest, which can lead to weight gain if dietary intake is not adjusted accordingly. A ketogenic diet, with its high-fat, moderate-protein, and low-carbohydrate approach, can be beneficial as it may help to increase metabolic efficiency and aid in weight management.

2. Loss of Muscle Mass (Sarcopenia)

Aging is often accompanied by reduced muscle mass and strength, a condition known as sarcopenia. This loss can affect mobility, balance, and overall health. Protein intake is crucial to combat muscle degradation; however, the ketogenic diet focuses on fat as the primary energy source, so careful attention must be paid to protein sources to ensure that adequate but not excessive amounts are consumed to preserve muscle mass without disrupting ketosis.

3. Hormonal Changes

Seniors experience significant hormonal changes that can impact energy levels, mood, and overall health. For example, insulin sensitivity typically decreases with age, which can increase the risk of type 2 diabetes. The ketogenic diet can help regulate blood sugar and insulin levels due to its low carbohydrate content, potentially mitigating some of the risks associated with these hormonal fluctuations.

4. Digestive and Absorption Issues

As we age, the body becomes less efficient at absorbing nutrients from food due to changes in digestive enzymes and gut health. This inefficiency necessitates more mindful choices about nutrient-dense foods and may warrant the incorporation of supplements. The ketogenic diet is rich in nutrient-dense foods like leafy greens, fatty fish, and nuts, which can help counteract these absorption issues.

5. Bone Density Decrease

A decrease in bone density, or osteoporosis, is common in seniors and poses a risk for fractures and other injuries. Calcium and vitamin D are essential for bone health; however, some ketogenic diets can be low in these nutrients if not adequately planned. Seniors must ensure they receive enough nutrients through their diet or supplements.

6. Changes in Cardiovascular Health

Heart health concerns increase with age; seniors must manage cholesterol and blood pressure levels to maintain cardiovascular health. The ketogenic diet has been shown to improve cholesterol levels by increasing HDL (good cholesterol) and decreasing LDL (bad cholesterol). However, the diet's high-fat content necessitates carefully selecting healthy fats to avoid exacerbating heart issues.

Understanding these physical changes and their interaction with dietary choices is essential for any senior considering a ketogenic diet. With careful planning and consideration of these age-related transformations, seniors can effectively adapt the ketogenic lifestyle to suit their changing bodies and enhance their overall health and well-being.

Gender-Specific Aging Effects

Aging affects men and women differently, influenced by biological, hormonal, and lifestyle factors. Understanding these gender-specific changes is essential for seniors to tailor the ketogenic diet to their needs effectively. This subchapter delves into the primary distinctions between how aging impacts men and women and provides insights on optimizing the ketogenic lifestyle accordingly.

1. Hormonal Changes

Men and women experience hormonal shifts differently as they age. Women undergo menopause, significantly decreasing estrogen and progesterone levels, affecting metabolism, mood, and bone density. Men experience a more gradual decline in testosterone, which can affect muscle mass, strength, and fat distribution. These hormonal changes can influence how each gender responds to the ketogenic diet, such as how they metabolize fats and proteins and their susceptibility to side effects like cholesterol fluctuations.

2. Metabolic Rate Variations

Women generally have a lower metabolic rate than men, which can slow further with age. This difference means that women may need to be more cautious with their calorie intake on a ketogenic diet to avoid potential weight gain. Conversely, men may require a higher protein intake to maintain muscle mass as they age, adjusting the typical macronutrient ratios in standard ketogenic diets.

3. Risk of Osteoporosis

Women are at a higher risk of developing osteoporosis after menopause due to the rapid decline in estrogen, a hormone that helps protect bone density. A ketogenic diet, sometimes low in calcium if not adequately managed, must be carefully planned to include bone-supporting nutrients. Both men and women should ensure adequate calcium and vitamin D intake, but women may need to be particularly vigilant about including these nutrients.

4. Heart Disease Risks

Men typically have a higher risk of heart disease earlier in life compared to women, though the risk for women increases and may surpass that of men post-menopause. The ketogenic diet has potential heart health benefits, such as improving cholesterol levels; however, the type of fats consumed needs careful consideration. Seniors, particularly post-menopausal women, should incorporate healthy fats from sources like avocados, nuts, and seeds to support cardiovascular health.

5. Body Composition and Fat Distribution

Due to hormonal influences, men and women tend to store fat differently. Men often accumulate visceral fat around the abdomen, which can be effectively reduced with a ketogenic diet. Women store more subcutaneous fat, particularly around the hips and thighs. These differences in fat storage and distribution can affect how quickly and effectively men and women see results from a ketogenic diet and may require adjustments in diet strategy.

6. Psychological and Emotional Health

Psychological and emotional responses to aging can also differ by gender and can be influenced by societal roles, personal expectations, and biological factors. A dietary program like keto should be paired with supportive networks and strategies that address these mental and emotional aspects, ensuring a holistic approach to health.

Recognizing and addressing these gender-specific aging effects within the context of a ketogenic diet helps ensure that seniors can customize their approach to meet their specific health needs and goals, enhancing the effectiveness of the diet and improving their overall quality of life.

The Ketogenic Diet's Role in Graceful Aging

Aging gracefully involves maintaining physical health, mental acuity, and overall quality of life as we age. With its unique nutritional approach, the ketogenic diet can significantly support these aspects of aging. This subchapter explores how the ketogenic diet can be leveraged to address common age-related challenges and enhance well-being among seniors.

1. Enhanced Cognitive Function

One of the most compelling benefits of the ketogenic diet for seniors is its potential to boost brain health. When carbohydrate intake is low, the brain can utilize ketones as an efficient alternative fuel source. This alternative energy can help protect against cognitive decline and support brain function. Studies suggest that the ketogenic diet may reduce the risk of neurodegenerative diseases like Alzheimer's and Parkinson's, providing a neuroprotective effect that is crucial for aging populations.

2. Increased Metabolic Efficiency

As we age, our metabolic rate naturally declines, which can lead to weight gain and associated health issues like type 2 diabetes and heart disease. The ketogenic diet helps to stabilize insulin levels and improve insulin sensitivity by reducing carbohydrate intake and increasing fat consumption. This metabolic shift helps manage body weight and reduces the risk of developing metabolic syndrome and other age-related metabolic diseases.

3. Improved Energy Levels

Many seniors experience fluctuations in energy levels, often impacted by poor diet and unstable blood sugar levels. The ketogenic diet helps maintain steady blood sugar levels by minimizing carbohydrate consumption, leading to more consistent energy throughout the day. This constant energy can improve physical activity levels and overall vitality, which is crucial to healthy aging.

4. Reduction in Inflammation

Chronic inflammation is a common issue in older adults and is associated with various age-related diseases, including arthritis, heart disease, and diabetes. Ketogenic diets have been shown to have anti-inflammatory properties due to the production of ketones and a reduction in inflammatory markers. This effect can help alleviate pain and stiffness associated with chronic inflammation, enhancing mobility and quality of life.

5. Support for Healthy Weight Management

Maintaining a healthy weight is often more challenging as we age due to decreased muscle mass and a slower metabolism. The high-fat, low-carb nature of the ketogenic diet promotes a feeling of fullness and satiety, which can prevent overeating and support weight management goals. Effective weight management is critical for physical health and reducing the burden on joints and the risk of many chronic conditions.

6. Promotion of Longevity and Autophagy

The ketogenic diet may promote longevity and the body's natural process of autophagy, where cells cleanse themselves of toxins and repair damage. This process prevents age-related cellular breakdown and promotes healthier, longer life spans.

By aligning with the body's changing needs, the ketogenic diet offers a promising approach to extending lifespan and enhancing the quality of life during the senior years. This dietary strategy empowers seniors to manage their health proactively, addressing preventive and reactive health needs through nutrition.

Chapter 2: Ketosis Fundamentals for Seniors

Exploring Ketosis: What It Is and Why It Matters

Ketosis is a metabolic state that is central to the ketogenic diet. It is particularly relevant for seniors looking to optimize their health and manage age-related conditions. This subchapter explains ketosis, how it works, and why it benefits seniors.

1. Understanding Ketosis

Ketosis occurs when the body switches its primary fuel source from carbohydrates to fats. This switch happens when carbohydrate intake is significantly reduced, typically below 50 grams daily, prompting the liver to convert fats into fatty acids and ketone bodies. The ketone bodies then serve as an alternative energy source for the brain and other organs. This process is a natural response to a low-carbohydrate intake and can be intentionally induced through a ketogenic diet.

2. The Process of Achieving Ketosis

Achieving ketosis involves adjusting your diet to reduce carbohydrate consumption while significantly increasing fat intake. This dietary shift can take several days to a few weeks as the body depletes its stored glucose and begins to ramp up ketone production. Seniors may notice symptoms such as fatigue, headaches, or mental fog during this transition, commonly called the "keto flu," which typically subsides as the body adapts.

3. Benefits of Ketosis for Seniors

Ketosis offers several health benefits that are particularly valuable for seniors:

- **Enhanced Cognitive Function**: Ketones provide a more efficient and consistent energy source for the brain, which may help improve cognitive function and protect against age-related mental decline.
- **Weight Management**: Ketosis naturally suppresses appetite and reduces calorie intake, helping seniors manage their weight more effectively.
- **Improved Energy Levels**: By stabilizing blood sugar levels, ketosis can improve energy levels throughout the day.

- **Reduced Inflammation**: Ketone bodies have anti-inflammatory properties that can help reduce chronic inflammation, a common issue in older adults.
- **Increased Insulin Sensitivity**: The ketogenic diet can improve insulin sensitivity, which is often reduced in seniors, helping to manage or prevent type 2 diabetes.

4. Why Ketosis Matters for Healthy Aging

Maintaining optimal health becomes increasingly important for seniors to preserve independence and quality of life. Ketosis supports physical health through mechanisms like weight control and reduced inflammation and bolsters mental health by improving mood and cognitive function. These benefits contribute to a more active, engaged, and fulfilling senior lifestyle.

Understanding the basics of ketosis and its impact on the body provides seniors with the knowledge needed to embark on a ketogenic diet with confidence. Knowing what to expect during the transition to ketosis and how to manage potential symptoms can help seniors achieve a smoother and more successful dietary adjustment. This foundational knowledge underscores the importance of ketosis in the broader context of healthy aging and overall wellness for seniors.

Safely Achieving and Maintaining Ketosis as a Senior

As seniors consider transitioning to a ketogenic diet, it's crucial to approach this change with an emphasis on safety and sustainability. This subchapter outlines practical steps and essential precautions for seniors to safely achieve and maintain ketosis, ensuring that the diet's benefits and health risks are minimized.

1. Consultation with Healthcare Professionals

The first step in safely adopting a ketogenic lifestyle is to consult with healthcare professionals. This is particularly important for seniors who may have pre-existing health conditions such as diabetes, cardiovascular diseases, or kidney issues. A medical professional can provide personalized advice and adjust any medications affected by dietary changes, ensuring the transition to ketosis is safe and tailored to individual health needs.

2. Gradual Transition into Ketosis

For seniors, a sudden switch to a high-fat, low-carbohydrate diet can shock the system. Gradually reducing carbohydrate intake over a few weeks can help mitigate symptoms associated with the "keto flu," such as headaches, fatigue, and nausea. This gradual approach allows the body to adjust more smoothly to burning fat for fuel instead of carbohydrates.

3. Monitoring Ketone Levels

Understanding and monitoring ketone levels can be essential to managing a ketogenic diet, especially in the beginning. Seniors can use blood, urine, or breath ketone testing methods to ensure they are in a state of ketosis. This monitoring helps adjust dietary intake to maintain an optimal level of ketosis that supports health without straining the body.

4. Adequate Hydration and Electrolyte Balance

Dehydration and electrolyte imbalances are common concerns when starting a ketogenic diet, as the diet can cause the body to excrete more water and electrolytes. Seniors should pay particular attention to consuming adequate fluids and electrolytes (such as sodium, potassium, and magnesium) to prevent these issues, which are particularly critical in older adults.

5. Nutrient-dense and Diverse Food Choices

While maintaining a focus on fats, seniors need to include a variety of nutrient-dense foods to avoid nutritional deficiencies. Incorporating a wide range of vegetables, quality proteins, and healthy fats ensures a balanced intake of vitamins and minerals necessary for overall health and well-being.

6. Regular Health Check-ups

Regular check-ups with a healthcare provider are essential while following a ketogenic diet. These visits can help track health markers like cholesterol levels, blood pressure, and blood sugar levels, adjusting the dietary approach based on these indicators.

7. Listening to the Body

Seniors must remain attentive to how their bodies respond to the ketogenic diet. Any persistent adverse symptoms or discomfort should prompt a reassessment of dietary choices and a consultation with a healthcare provider. Listening to the body's signals is crucial in maintaining ketosis and overall health.

By following these guidelines, seniors can safely enjoy the benefits of the ketogenic diet, such as improved metabolic health, increased mental clarity, and better energy levels, all while minimizing potential risks associated with dietary changes in older age.

Overview of Ketogenic Diet Variants

The ketogenic diet is versatile, with several variants that cater to different dietary preferences and health goals. This subchapter provides an overview of the most common types of ketogenic diets, explaining their unique characteristics and how they can be adapted to suit the needs of seniors. Understanding these variants allows for a more personalized approach to keto, enhancing its effectiveness and sustainability.

1. Standard Ketogenic Diet (SKD)

The Standard Ketogenic Diet is the most basic and widely used form of keto. It typically comprises 70-75% fat, 20-25% protein, and 5-10% carbohydrates. This ratio ensures that the body enters and maintains a state of ketosis, where it burns fat as its primary source of energy. For seniors, the SKD can be beneficial for its simplicity and effectiveness in weight management and blood sugar control.

2. High-Protein Ketogenic Diet (HPKD)

The High-Protein Ketogenic Diet modifies the standard ratio to include more protein, usually around 60% fat, 35% protein, and 5% carbohydrates. This variant can benefit seniors concerned about muscle loss, as the increased protein intake helps preserve muscle mass. However, monitoring protein intake carefully ensures it doesn't interfere with maintaining ketosis.

3. Cyclical Ketogenic Diet (CKD)

The Cyclical Ketogenic Diet involves periods of higher-carb refeeds, such as five ketogenic days followed by two high-carb days. Athletes often use this approach to replenish glycogen stores in muscles. Still, it can also benefit seniors who need periodic carbohydrate intake to support intense physical activity or provide a psychological break from strict keto.

4. Targeted Ketogenic Diet (TKD)

The Targeted Ketogenic Diet allows for adding carbohydrates around workouts. For active seniors, TKD can help maintain energy levels during exercise by providing a quick source of glucose that fuels muscles. This variant requires timing carbohydrate intake carefully to ensure it does not disrupt ketosis more than necessary.

5. Lazy Keto

Lazy Keto focuses solely on carb intake without precise tracking of other macronutrients. Seniors might find this variant appealing for its simplicity, as it reduces the need to track everything they eat. Lazy Keto can be effective for those primarily interested in the benefits of reduced carb consumption without the stricter aspects of standard keto tracking.

6. Strict Keto

Strict Keto involves meticulous tracking of all macronutrients to ensure that daily percentages are met precisely. This variant can benefit seniors who need precise dietary control to manage specific health conditions, such as diabetes or neurological diseases. It requires more diligence but can provide significant benefits when strict adherence is necessary.

Each ketogenic diet variant offers different advantages and can be tailored to meet individual health needs, preferences, and lifestyle considerations. Seniors considering a ketogenic diet should start with a clear understanding of these options and consult with healthcare providers to determine which variant aligns best with their health goals. While it may take some experimentation to find the most suitable approach, the flexibility of the ketogenic diet makes it a viable and beneficial option for healthy aging.

Practical Tips for Adopting Keto in Senior Years

Adopting a ketogenic lifestyle can be a significant adjustment, especially for seniors. This subchapter offers practical tips and strategies to ease the transition into a ketogenic diet, ensuring a positive, sustainable change for seniors looking to enhance their health and well-being. These tips are designed to make the keto journey approachable for beginners while providing enough depth to ensure success and longevity on the diet.

1. Start with a Clear Plan

Having a clear, structured plan can make the transition to a ketogenic diet much smoother. Consult a healthcare provider or dietitian to tailor the keto approach to your health needs. Plan your meals weekly, including what to eat and when to avoid the temptation of reaching for non-keto-friendly foods.

2. Ease into the Diet Gradually

A sudden switch to a high-fat, low-carb diet can be challenging for seniors. Start by gradually reducing carbohydrate intake and increasing fat and protein over a few weeks. This slower approach can help mitigate the initial side effects often associated with the transition to ketosis, such as the keto flu.

3. Focus on Nutrient-Dense Foods

Choose high-quality, nutrient-dense foods that provide vitamins, minerals, and antioxidants. Incorporate a variety of low-carb vegetables, fatty fish, meats, and healthy fats like avocados and olive oil. Seniors must focus on foods rich in nutrients supporting bone health, cardiovascular health, and cognitive function.

4. Stay Hydrated and Mindful of Electrolytes

Hydration is crucial on a ketogenic diet as it can naturally lead to a loss of fluids and electrolytes. Drink plenty of water and add electrolytes like sodium, potassium, and magnesium to your diet. This is especially important for seniors, who are more susceptible to dehydration and electrolyte imbalances.

5. Keep Track of Your Health Metrics

Monitor your health metrics regularly, including blood sugar levels, cholesterol, and blood pressure, particularly if you have underlying health conditions. Based on these metrics, adjustments to the diet may be necessary. Keeping track can help ensure the diet has the intended positive effects on your health.

6. Prepare for Social and Emotional Adjustments

Adopting a new diet can affect more than just your eating habits; it can also impact your social life and emotional well-being. Prepare for how you'll handle social gatherings and explain your dietary choices to friends and family to garner support. Also, consider joining support groups or online communities of people who are also living a ketogenic lifestyle.

7. Regular Physical Activity

Combine the diet with regular physical activity you enjoy and can consistently perform. Activities like walking, swimming, or yoga can complement the health benefits of keto, such as weight loss and improved metabolic health while enhancing mobility and balance.

8. Consult Resources and Continue Learning

Stay informed by consulting various resources such as books, reputable websites, and keto-focused cooking classes. Continuous learning will help you stay motivated, provide new recipe ideas, and keep you updated on the latest research about keto for seniors.

By following these practical tips, seniors can adopt and maintain a ketogenic lifestyle that enhances their quality of life and supports their health goals. Each step should be personalized to fit individual health statuses and lifestyle preferences, making the journey into keto rewarding and enjoyable.

Cultivating a Supportive Keto Community

Adopting a ketogenic lifestyle can be a significant change, especially for seniors. Having a supportive community can make this transition smoother and more enjoyable. This subchapter explores ways to cultivate a support network that can offer encouragement, share experiences, and provide valuable advice as you navigate the challenges and triumphs of maintaining a ketogenic diet.

1. Engage with Online Communities

One of the easiest ways to find support is through online forums and social media groups dedicated to the ketogenic lifestyle. These platforms are rich with resources, recipes, and personal stories that can offer inspiration and practical advice. For seniors, especially those with mobility limitations, online communities provide a valuable touchpoint with others who share similar goals and challenges without needing to leave home.

2. Attend Local Meetups and Support Groups

Check for local keto meetups, cooking classes, or support groups in your area. These gatherings can be great opportunities to meet like-minded individuals, share experiences, and learn new tips and recipes. For seniors, these groups can also offer a sense of belonging and community engagement, which is essential for overall well-being.

3. Involve Family and Friends

Share your keto journey with your family and friends. Educating them about your diet can help them better support you, especially during family gatherings and meals. They can be your closest allies in maintaining your dietary goals and might join you in adopting a healthier lifestyle, creating a shared experience that enhances your relationship.

4. Partner with a Buddy

Having a keto buddy can significantly enhance your motivation and commitment. This could be a friend on the diet or someone you meet in one of your support groups. You can plan meals together, share resources, and keep each other accountable, making the journey less daunting and more enjoyable.

5. Consult with Dietitians and Healthcare Providers

Build a supportive network that includes professionals like dietitians and healthcare providers knowledgeable about the ketogenic diet. They can offer expert advice tailored to your specific health needs and help you navigate any medical concerns. This professional support is crucial for seniors to ensure the diet is followed safely and effectively.

6. Participate in Workshops and Seminars

Look for workshops, seminars, or webinars about the ketogenic diet. These educational opportunities are not only informative but also a great way to meet others who are interested in keto. Many organizations and health clinics offer sessions tailored to seniors, focusing on how keto can be adapted to meet age-related nutritional needs.

7. Volunteer and Lead

Once you are comfortable with your knowledge of keto, consider volunteering or leading a group yourself. Sharing your experiences and what you've learned can be incredibly fulfilling. It also helps others who are just starting, reinforcing your understanding and commitment to the ketogenic lifestyle.

By cultivating these connections and resources, seniors can build a supportive keto community that enhances their diet experience, provides emotional and practical support, and contributes to successful, long-term adherence to a ketogenic lifestyle.

Chapter 3: Benefits and Risks of Keto for Seniors

Advantages of Keto in Senior Health

The ketogenic diet offers numerous health benefits, particularly advantageous for seniors. This subchapter delves into how adopting a keto lifestyle can positively impact senior health, from enhancing metabolic efficiency to improving cognitive function.

1. Enhanced Cognitive Function

One of the most notable benefits of the ketogenic diet is its potential to boost brain health. For seniors, this is crucial as cognitive decline often accompanies aging. Ketones, produced during ketosis, provide an efficient energy source for the brain, which may help improve memory, clarity, and cognitive resilience. Research suggests that the ketogenic diet may also reduce the risk of neurodegenerative diseases like Alzheimer's and Parkinson's.

2. Weight Management

As metabolism slows with age, seniors often find it challenging to maintain a healthy weight. The ketogenic diet aids in weight management by increasing satiety and decreasing hunger, thanks to its high-fat and moderate-protein content. This can help seniors maintain a healthy weight, which is vital for reducing the risk of several chronic diseases such as type 2 diabetes, heart disease, and certain cancers.

3. Improved Insulin Sensitivity

Many seniors struggle with insulin resistance, which can lead to type 2 diabetes. By reducing carbohydrate intake, the ketogenic diet helps to lower blood sugar levels and improve insulin sensitivity. This dietary adjustment can benefit seniors, helping them manage or prevent diabetes.

4. Increased Energy and Mobility

Stable energy levels are crucial for maintaining an active lifestyle in older age. The ketogenic diet stabilizes blood sugar, improving energy levels throughout the day. This energy increase can enhance seniors' mobility and independence, allowing them to engage more in physical activities and enjoy a higher quality of life.

5. Reduction in Inflammation

Chronic inflammation is joint in older adults and is associated with numerous age-related diseases. The ketogenic diet has natural anti-inflammatory properties that can help reduce inflammation and alleviate symptoms associated with inflammatory conditions such as arthritis. This benefit can lead to improved mobility and less discomfort.

6. Support for Heart Health

Cardiovascular health is a significant concern for seniors. The ketogenic diet can improve heart health by reducing triglycerides and bad LDL cholesterol while increasing good HDL cholesterol. However, choosing healthy fats and monitoring overall dietary balance is essential to realizing these cardiovascular benefits.

7. Promotion of Longevity

Emerging research suggests that the ketogenic diet could extend lifespan and improve health by reducing oxidative stress and enhancing cellular repair processes. For seniors, this could mean living longer and enjoying better health and functionality in later years.

By incorporating the ketogenic diet into their lifestyle, seniors can leverage these advantages to address specific age-related health issues and enhance their overall well-being and vitality.

Potential Risks and How to Mitigate Them

While the ketogenic diet offers numerous benefits for seniors, it also comes with potential risks that must be carefully managed. This subchapter explores these risks and provides strategies for seniors to mitigate them, ensuring a safe and healthy experience with the ketogenic lifestyle.

1. Nutritional Deficiencies

The restrictive nature of the ketogenic diet can lead to deficiencies in specific vitamins and minerals, mainly if the diet is not well-planned. Seniors might be at risk of low intakes of fiber, calcium, vitamin D, and B vitamins.

- **Mitigation Strategy**: Diversify your diet within the keto constraints by including various nutrient-rich foods. Leafy greens, low-carb vegetables, nuts, seeds, and keto-approved dairy can provide essential nutrients. Consider supplementing with vitamins and minerals as recommended by a healthcare provider.

2. Dehydration and Electrolyte Imbalance

Keto can increase fluid and electrolyte loss, especially in the early stages. This can be a significant concern for seniors already prone to dehydration.

- **Mitigation Strategy**: Increase fluid intake and consider adding a balanced electrolyte supplement. Regularly consuming broth or bouillon can also help maintain sodium levels, which is crucial for electrolyte balance.

3. Kidney Stones and Renal Health

There is a potential risk of kidney stones and other renal complications from a high intake of animal fats and proteins, which are common in a poorly managed ketogenic diet.

- **Mitigation Strategy**: Ensure a healthy balance of fat sources, incorporating more plant-based fats and lean proteins. Stay hydrated and monitor protein intake to align with individual health needs, reducing the burden on kidneys.

4. Heart Health Concerns

A high intake of saturated fats, often found in a ketogenic diet, can raise concerns about heart health, particularly for seniors with existing cardiovascular conditions.

- **Mitigation Strategy**: Focus on healthy fats like those from avocados, nuts, seeds, and olive oil. Regular check-ups to monitor cholesterol and triglyceride levels can help manage and adjust dietary fats to support heart health.

5. Bone Health

The ketogenic diet can affect bone health due to a reduced intake of fruits and certain vegetables, essential sources of vitamins and minerals like calcium and vitamin K.

- **Mitigation Strategy**: Include keto-friendly sources of these nutrients, such as leafy greens and full-fat dairy products. Engage in regular weight-bearing exercise to strengthen bones and enhance calcium absorption.

6. Gastrointestinal Discomfort

Changes in diet composition can lead to constipation or diarrhea. This is particularly disruptive for seniors, who may already have sensitive digestive systems.

- **Mitigation Strategy**: Increase fiber intake through low-carb vegetables and consider a dietary supplement. Proper hydration also plays a crucial role in maintaining digestive health.

7. Social and Psychological Impact

Adhering to a strict diet can sometimes lead to social isolation or frustration, especially when dining out or participating in social events.

- **Mitigation Strategy**: Plan for social gatherings by identifying keto-friendly options or bringing your dishes. Engage with keto support groups, both online and in-person, to share experiences and tips for navigating social situations.

By recognizing and proactively managing these potential risks, seniors can safely enjoy the benefits of the ketogenic diet while minimizing the downsides, leading to a healthier and more enjoyable senior life.

Strategies for Managing Side Effects

While the ketogenic diet offers significant health benefits for seniors, transitioning to and maintaining it can sometimes lead to side effects. This subchapter provides strategies for effectively managing these side effects, ensuring seniors can reap the benefits of keto without undue discomfort or health risks.

1. Managing Keto Flu

One of the most common side effects when starting the ketogenic diet is the "keto flu," characterized by symptoms like fatigue, headaches, and irritability. This occurs as the body adjusts to burning fat instead of carbohydrates.

- **Mitigation Strategy**: Increase salt and water intake to manage electrolyte imbalances that can cause keto flu symptoms. Consuming bone broth and using salt generously in meals can help replenish sodium levels. Also, ease into the diet gradually to give your body time to adjust to the new energy source.

2. Preventing Constipation

A decrease in fiber intake due to lower consumption of fruits and certain vegetables can lead to constipation on a ketogenic diet.

- **Mitigation Strategy**: Incorporate more low-carb, high-fiber vegetables like broccoli, cauliflower, and leafy greens into your diet. Staying hydrated is also crucial, as water helps fiber function effectively in the digestive system. If necessary, consider a fiber supplement that is low in carbohydrates.

3. Avoiding Dehydration and Electrolyte Imbalances

The ketogenic diet increases fluid excretion, leading to dehydration and an imbalance of sodium, potassium, and magnesium electrolytes.

- **Mitigation Strategy**: Drink plenty of water throughout the day. Supplement with electrolytes if needed, particularly if you experience symptoms like muscle cramps or general weakness. Electrolyte supplements designed explicitly for ketogenic dieters are available and can be a convenient way to maintain balance.

4. Handling Increased Cholesterol Levels

Some individuals may experience elevated cholesterol levels when on a high-fat diet, which can concern heart health.

- **Mitigation Strategy**: Choose healthier fats, such as those from avocados, nuts, seeds, and olive oil, rather than relying heavily on saturated fats from red meat and butter. Regularly monitoring your cholesterol levels through blood tests will help you and your healthcare provider make necessary adjustments to your diet.

5. Addressing Nutrient Deficiencies

Restricting certain food groups can lead to deficiencies in vitamins and minerals, including vitamin D, calcium, and specific B vitamins.

- **Mitigation Strategy**: Plan meals to include a variety of nutrient-dense foods. Supplements may be necessary to meet the nutritional needs of seniors. Consult a healthcare provider to determine which supplements are appropriate based on your health profile and dietary intake.

6. Coping with Social and Emotional Challenges

Adhering to a strict diet can sometimes lead to feelings of isolation or frustration during social events where food choices are limited.

- **Mitigation Strategy**: Communicate your dietary needs with hosts in advance or offer to bring a dish to share that fits within your dietary constraints. Find support from keto-friendly communities online or locally where you can share experiences and gain encouragement.

By implementing these strategies, seniors can mitigate the side effects associated with the ketogenic diet, making their transition to and maintenance of this lifestyle more comfortable and sustainable.

Lifestyle Integration: Making Keto a Sustainable Choice

For seniors, integrating the ketogenic diet into everyday life is about more than managing nutrition; it's about making it a sustainable, enjoyable part of their lifestyle. This subchapter provides strategies for seamlessly incorporating keto into their daily routines, ensuring it enhances their quality of life and remains a feasible long-term option.

1. Personalizing the Diet to Fit Individual Preferences

Keto is not one-size-fits-all. Tailor the diet to include foods you enjoy and avoid those you dislike. Personalization can prevent dietary fatigue and make the ketogenic lifestyle more enjoyable and sustainable.

- **Strategy**: Experiment with keto-friendly substitutes for favorite non-keto foods. Use almond flour for baking, cauliflower rice instead of grain rice, and explore the variety of low-carb snack options available.

2. Simplifying Meal Preparation

Meal preparation can be a hurdle, especially for seniors. Simplifying this process can help integrate keto more smoothly into everyday life.

- **Strategy**: Batch cook meals to reduce daily cooking time. Invest in a slow or pressure cooker to make meal preparation more accessible and efficient. Prepare and freeze several meals in advance to have ready-to-eat options on hand.

3. Incorporating Keto into Social and Family Gatherings

Dietary restrictions shouldn't isolate you from social interactions or family events, which are vital for emotional well-being.

- **Strategy**: Plan for gatherings by bringing your keto-friendly dishes to share. This ensures you have something appropriate to eat and introduces others to your lifestyle. Communicate openly with family and friends about your dietary needs to foster understanding and support.

4. Adjusting for Physical Activity Levels

Physical activity is essential to a healthy lifestyle, especially for seniors. Keto can affect energy levels, so adjusting your diet based on your activity level is vital.

- **Strategy**: If you are active, you may need to increase your carbohydrate or protein intake during physical activities slightly. Consider the targeted ketogenic diet (TKD) approach for better performance and recovery.

5. Regular Monitoring and Adjustment

As your body changes, so too might your dietary needs. Regularly reassessing the effectiveness of your diet and making necessary adjustments ensures continued health benefits.

- **Strategy**: Schedule regular check-ups with your healthcare provider to monitor health markers. Adjust your diet based on these outcomes and any changes in your health status or physical activity levels.

6. Educational Commitment

Continuously educating yourself about the ketogenic diet and its developments can help you make informed decisions and keep your routine fresh.

- **Strategy**: Stay informed about new keto research, recipes, and resources. Subscribe to keto newsletters, follow keto food blogs, and participate in community forums.

7. Psychological Resilience

Mental and emotional adaptability is critical when integrating any significant lifestyle change, including dietary ones.

- **Strategy**: Practice mindfulness and stress reduction techniques such as yoga or meditation to maintain mental and emotional balance. Acknowledge and celebrate your progress to boost motivation.

By adopting these strategies, seniors can successfully integrate the ketogenic diet into their lifestyle naturally and sustainably, enhancing their overall health and allowing them to enjoy the long-term benefits of keto.

Addressing Common Questions and Concerns

When seniors consider adopting the ketogenic diet, they often have a variety of questions and concerns about how it will affect their health and daily living. This subchapter addresses these common inquiries, providing clear, concise answers and reassurances to help seniors feel more confident about their dietary choices.

1. Is the ketogenic diet safe for seniors with existing health conditions?

Many seniors worry about how the ketogenic diet will interact with conditions like heart disease, diabetes, and hypertension.

- **Answer**: The ketogenic diet can be safe for seniors with existing health conditions, but it should be approached with care. It is essential to consult with healthcare providers to tailor the diet to individual health needs and to monitor the condition closely while on the diet.

2. Will I get enough fiber on a ketogenic diet?

Concerns about fiber intake are common due to the low-carb diet, which limits traditional sources of fiber like grains and some fruits.

- **Answer**: Yes, you can still get enough fiber on a ketogenic diet by incorporating low-carb vegetables like leafy greens, broccoli, and Brussels sprouts, as well as seeds and nuts. Fiber supplements can also be used if necessary.

3. How can I manage the social implications of dietary restrictions?

Seniors are often concerned about how their dietary choices will affect social interactions and participation in family gatherings.

- **Answer**: Communicate openly with friends and family about your dietary needs. Offer to bring dishes to gatherings that align with your diet. Most importantly, focus on the social aspect of gatherings rather than just the food.

4. What if I experience significant side effects or don't like the diet?

It's common to worry about adverse effects or simply not enjoying the food choices available on the ketogenic diet.

- **Answer**: Start with a trial period to see how your body reacts and adjust the diet as needed with the help of a nutritionist or dietitian. Numerous keto recipes cater to various taste preferences, and many enjoy the richness and variety of the diet.

5. Can I still eat out or travel on a ketogenic diet?

Maintaining dietary restrictions while eating out or traveling is a concern for many seniors.

- **Answer**: With planning, you can maintain your ketogenic diet. Research restaurants in advance to find those that offer keto-friendly options. Pack some keto snacks when traveling, and consider access to kitchen facilities where you can prepare your meals if necessary.

6. How will the ketogenic diet affect my medication needs?

Seniors often take various medications, and changes in diet can affect how these medications work.

- **Answer**: Some seniors may find that they need adjustments in their medication dosages, especially for conditions like diabetes or hypertension, as the ketogenic diet can alter blood sugar and blood pressure levels. Always discuss any dietary changes with your healthcare provider, who can help adjust your medications as needed.

7. Is it necessary to exercise while on the ketogenic diet?

Exercise is vital for overall health, but seniors often question how it fits into a ketogenic lifestyle.

- **Answer**: While the ketogenic diet can be beneficial on its own, combining it with exercise can enhance its health benefits, particularly for weight management and improved metabolic health. Choose activities you enjoy and can sustain, such as walking, swimming, or yoga, and consult a professional to tailor exercise to your capabilities and needs.

By addressing these common questions and concerns, seniors can better understand the ketogenic diet and feel more prepared to make informed decisions about integrating it into their lifestyle.

Inspirational Senior Success Stories

Adopting a new dietary lifestyle like the ketogenic diet can be a significant challenge, especially for seniors. However, real-life success stories can serve as powerful motivation, illustrating the tangible benefits and transformative potential of keto in the lives of older adults. This subchapter shares several inspirational stories from seniors who have successfully integrated the ketogenic diet into their lives, showcasing the positive impact on their health and overall well-being.

1. John's Journey to Improved Heart Health

At 72, John was struggling with high cholesterol and hypertension, conditions common in his family. Despite various medications, his numbers were barely under control. After adopting a ketogenic diet under his doctor's supervision, John not only saw a significant drop in his cholesterol levels but also reduced his hypertension medication. Six months into his keto journey, John reported feeling more energetic and enjoying life more than he had in years.

2. Mary's Victory Over Type 2 Diabetes

Mary, a 68-year-old retiree, was diagnosed with type 2 diabetes and faced the daily routine of managing her blood sugar with medication and frequent insulin injections. Encouraged by her daughter, she started a ketogenic diet, focusing on healthy fats, moderate protein, and low carbs. Within a year, Mary's blood sugar levels stabilized to the point where her doctor significantly reduced her medications. Mary now enjoys gardening without the constant worry about her blood sugar.

3. Alice's Return to Cognitive Clarity

Alice began noticing her memory wasn't as sharp as it used to be at 70. Concerned about cognitive decline, she researched lifestyle changes that could help and decided to try the ketogenic diet. The high-fat, low-carb diet helped her lose some unwanted weight and cleared the fog she felt every morning. Alice's improved cognitive function has allowed her to take up new hobbies like writing and birdwatching, which require attention to detail and sharp memory.

4. Bob's Rebound from Sarcopenia

After a minor fall that resulted in a fracture, Bob, aged 75, was diagnosed with sarcopenia, which is the loss of skeletal muscle mass and strength. Determined to regain strength and mobility, Bob combined a high-protein ketogenic diet with a light resistance training regimen. Six months later, Bob improved his muscle mass, regained full mobility, and reduced his fall risk, allowing him to continue volunteering at the local library.

5. Sandra's Social Revival

Sandra, 65, felt isolated because her dietary restrictions made social gatherings challenging. After starting a ketogenic diet, she was initially worried it would worsen her social life. However, Sandra found a local keto support group and made new friends with similar dietary goals. They often exchange recipes and dine together at keto-friendly restaurants. Sandra's new social circle has dramatically enhanced her emotional well-being and made her dietary changes more enjoyable and sustainable.

These stories demonstrate the health benefits of the ketogenic diet for seniors and highlight the diet's potential to enhance quality of life in various ways. By seeing others who have faced similar challenges and triumphed, seniors can be inspired to embark on their ketogenic journey with renewed confidence and hope.

Chapter 4: Senior-Specific Keto Shopping Insights

Essential Keto-Friendly Foods

Understanding which foods to incorporate into their diet is crucial for seniors embarking on the ketogenic journey. This subchapter provides a comprehensive list of essential keto-friendly foods that are beneficial for maintaining ketosis and cater to the nutritional needs of older adults. These foods help ensure a balanced intake of nutrients while adhering to the low-carb, high-fat principles of the ketogenic diet.

1. Healthy Fats

Healthy fats are the cornerstone of the ketogenic diet, providing the majority of daily caloric intake and helping to keep you satiated.

- **Avocados**: Rich in monounsaturated fats and very low in carbohydrates, avocados are also a good source of fiber and potassium, essential for heart and muscle health.
- **Olive Oil**: Excellent for dressings or drizzling over dishes, olive oil is high in oleic acid, a heart-healthy fat.
- **Coconut Oil**: Contains medium-chain triglycerides (MCTs), which are processed differently by the body, potentially helping to maintain ketosis.
- **Butter and Cream**: Full-fat dairy products provide a good amount of fat with minimal carbs, but they should be consumed in moderation.

2. Proteins

Proteins are vital for preserving muscle mass and are significant for seniors in preventing sarcopenia (muscle loss associated with aging).

- **Fatty Fish**: Options like salmon, trout, mackerel, and sardines are low in carbohydrates and high in omega-3 fatty acids, which are crucial for brain and heart health.
- **Eggs**: A versatile protein source, eggs are low in carbs and one of the best sources of choline, a nutrient that supports brain function.
- **Grass-Fed Meats**: Beef, pork, and lamb are higher in omega-3 fatty acids than their grain-fed counterparts and do not contain carbs.

3. Low-Carb Vegetables

Vegetables are essential to a balanced diet, providing vitamins, minerals, and fiber without too many carbs.

- **Leafy Greens**: Spinach, kale, and other leafy greens are high in iron and vitamins A, C, and K.
- **Cruciferous Vegetables**: Broccoli, cauliflower, and Brussels sprouts offer fiber and are rich in nutrients with minimal impact on blood sugar.
- **Bell Peppers and Zucchini**: Provide essential vitamins and make great low-carb alternatives in various dishes.

4. Dairy and Cheese

Cheese and other high-fat dairy products can be good sources of calcium and protein.

- **Cheddar, Feta, and Mozzarella**: These cheeses are low in carbs and high in fat, making them excellent for keto.
- **Full-fat Greek Yogurt and Cottage Cheese** Can be consumed in moderation for their probiotic and protein benefits.

5. Nuts and Seeds

Nuts and seeds are great for snacks or adding crunch to meals.

- **Almonds, Walnuts, and Flaxseeds**: These are high in healthy fats, omega-3 fatty acids, and fiber, which are beneficial for heart health and digestion.
- **Chia Seeds**: Exceptionally high in fiber and omega-3 fatty acids, they are versatile and can be added to smoothies or used as a pudding base.

6. Beverages

Proper hydration is crucial, especially for seniors.

- **Water**: Should be consumed liberally.
- **Bone Broth**: Offers hydration, minerals, and other nutrients beneficial for joint and digestive health.
- **Unsweetened Tea and Coffee**: These are keto-friendly and can be enjoyed without additives.

By incorporating these essential keto-friendly foods into their diet, seniors can ensure they receive the nutrients necessary for a healthy lifestyle while effectively managing their carbohydrate intake to maintain ketosis.

Supplement Guidance for Optimal Health

While the ketogenic diet provides many nutritional benefits, certain nutrients might be less abundant due to the restrictions on fruits, certain vegetables, and whole grains. This can be particularly crucial for seniors with specific dietary needs to maintain optimal health. This subchapter offers guidance on supplements supporting a healthy ketogenic lifestyle for seniors, ensuring they receive all necessary nutrients.

1. Multivitamins

A broad-spectrum multivitamin can help fill nutritional gaps in a keto diet, providing essential vitamins and minerals that might be under-consumed.

- **Consideration**: Look for a multivitamin without added sugars or excessive fillers that provide a balanced range of nutrients suitable for seniors.

2. Electrolytes

The ketogenic diet can increase electrolyte excretion. Supplementing electrolytes is crucial to avoid imbalances that can cause physical symptoms like muscle cramps or fatigue.

- **Key Electrolytes**: Sodium, potassium, and magnesium.
- **Usage Tips**: Choose easily absorbable supplements that do not contain added sugars or carbohydrates.

3. Omega-3 Fatty Acids

Omega-3 supplements, such as fish oil or krill oil, are beneficial for heart and brain health, which are critical for seniors.

- **Benefits**: Supports cardiovascular health, reduces inflammation, and may help lower levels of depression.
- **Dosage**: Consult with a healthcare provider to determine the appropriate dosage, especially if you regularly consume fatty fish.

4. Vitamin D and Calcium

These are important for bone health, especially seniors at increased risk of osteoporosis and fractures.

- **Vitamin D**: Helps improve calcium absorption and boosts immune function.
- **Calcium**: Maintains bone density and overall skeletal health.

- **Recommendation**: Seniors may require higher levels of these nutrients and should consider supplements if dietary intake is insufficient.

5. Fiber

A common issue with the ketogenic diet is getting enough fiber, which is crucial for digestive health.

- **Fiber Types**: Soluble and insoluble fiber supplements can help support regular bowel movements and prevent constipation.
- **Product Choice**: Psyllium husk, flaxseed, and chia seeds are good options with low net carbs.

6. MCT Oil

Medium-chain triglyceride (MCT) oil is a supplement that can help increase ketone levels and provide a quick energy source.

- **Benefits**: Supports cognitive function and energy levels without disrupting ketosis.
- **Usage**: Start with a small dosage to assess tolerance and increase gradually as needed.

7. Probiotics

Gut health is essential for overall wellness, particularly in seniors, as digestion can become less efficient with age.

- **Advantages**: It helps maintain a healthy gut microbiota, which is crucial for digestion and immune function.
- **Selection**: Choose a probiotic with various strains and a high colony-forming unit (CFU) count to ensure effectiveness.

Before starting any supplement, seniors must consult with their healthcare provider to ensure compatibility with their health status and other medications. This personalized approach helps maximize the benefits of the ketogenic diet while minimizing potential risks associated with nutritional deficiencies.

List of Foods to Avoid

For seniors following the ketogenic diet, it is crucial to be aware of foods that can disrupt ketosis, hinder health goals, or provide little nutritional value. This subchapter outlines specific foods that should typically be avoided or significantly limited to maintain the effectiveness of the ketogenic lifestyle and support overall health.

1. High-Carb Foods

The ketogenic diet requires a significant reduction in carbohydrate intake. Foods high in carbs can prevent the body from entering or maintaining ketosis.

- **Sugary Foods**: Candy, ice cream, and other sweets are high in sugar and carbs.
- **Grains**: Wheat-based products, rice, pasta, and cereals should be avoided as they are high in carbohydrates.
- **Starchy Vegetables**: Potatoes, yams, and other starchy vegetables are high in carbs and should be limited.
- **Legumes**: Beans, lentils, and chickpeas are nutritious but high in carbs and can disrupt ketosis.

2. Processed Foods

While some processed foods are marketed as low-carb or keto-friendly, many contain unhealthy fats, excessive sodium, and other additives that are not conducive to overall health.

- **Processed Meats**: Sausages, hot dogs, and deli meats often contain preservatives and hidden carbs.
- **Snack Foods**: Chips, crackers, and other packaged snacks typically have refined oils and artificial ingredients.
- **Diet and Low-Fat Products**: These often contain high amounts of sugars and unhealthy additives to improve taste and texture after fat is reduced or removed.

3. Unhealthy Fats

While fats are a vital component of the ketogenic diet, the type of fat consumed is crucial for maintaining health, especially for seniors.

- **Trans Fats**: In margarine, shortening, and some processed foods, trans fats can increase harmful cholesterol levels and are linked to heart disease.

- **High Omega-6 Vegetable Oils**: Corn oil, sunflower oil, and soybean oil are high in omega-6 fatty acids, which can contribute to inflammation if not balanced with omega-3s.

4. Sugary Beverages

Sugary drinks are high in carbohydrates and offer no nutritional benefit, making them incompatible with a ketogenic diet.

- **Soda**: Regular sodas, and even some diet sodas, can contain hidden sugars or artificial sweeteners that may affect blood sugar and insulin levels.
- **Fruit Juices**: Although they come from fruit, juices are concentrated sources of sugar and lack the fiber that whole fruits provide.

5. Artificial Sweeteners

While some artificial sweeteners are keto-friendly, others can cause sugar cravings and may impact gut health or blood sugar stability.

- **Avoid**: Aspartame, sucralose, and saccharin may affect some individuals' insulin and blood sugar levels.
- **Preferred Options**: Stevia, erythritol, and monk fruit are generally recognized as safe and minimal in carb content.

6. Alcohol

Moderation is vital with alcohol, especially on a ketogenic diet, as many alcoholic drinks contain hidden sugars and can impede liver function and fat metabolism.

- **Limit**: Beer, sweet wines, and cocktails often contain significant carbohydrates and can disrupt ketosis.

Awareness of these foods and avoiding them as much as possible can help seniors maintain a healthy ketogenic diet that promotes ketosis, supports their dietary goals, and contributes to overall health. Adjusting nutritional habits can be challenging, but focusing on nutritious, whole foods and avoiding these potential pitfalls will significantly enhance the benefits of the ketogenic lifestyle for seniors.

Chapter 5: Physical Fitness and Keto Adaptation

The Importance of Exercise for Seniors on Keto

Integrating regular physical activity is crucial for seniors adopting a ketogenic diet. This subchapter explores why exercise is essential for seniors on a ketogenic diet and how it complements the nutritional aspects of keto to improve quality of life.

1. Enhanced Metabolic Health

Exercise boosts metabolism, which can enhance the effects of the ketogenic diet on weight management and metabolic health. This combination is particularly effective for seniors in managing or preventing conditions like type 2 diabetes and metabolic syndrome. Regular physical activity helps increase insulin sensitivity, which is beneficial because insulin resistance increases with age.

2. Improved Muscle Mass and Strength

Muscle mass naturally decreases with age, a condition known as sarcopenia. This loss can lead to reduced mobility and an increased risk of falls and fractures. Exercise, especially strength training, can help mitigate and rebuild muscle loss. Combined with a ketogenic diet, which can help preserve muscle mass, exercise ensures seniors maintain strength and functionality.

3. Enhanced Cognitive Function

There is growing evidence that physical activity has neuroprotective benefits. Exercise increases blood flow to the brain, which can help maintain cognitive functions and potentially slow the progression of cognitive decline. Coupled with the ketogenic diet, which has potential benefits for brain health, exercise can play a critical role in maintaining cognitive abilities in seniors.

4. Improved Cardiovascular Health

Regular exercise strengthens the heart and improves circulation, vital for cardiovascular health. The ketogenic diet's impact on reducing inflammation and potentially improving lipid profiles can enhance cardiovascular health when combined with aerobic activities like walking, cycling, or swimming.

5. Bone Density and Joint Health

Weight-bearing and resistance exercises are crucial for maintaining bone density and joint health. The lower intake of certain minerals, like calcium, counteracts bone density loss in a ketogenic diet. Exercise also helps maintain joint flexibility and can reduce the pain associated with arthritis.

6. Mental Health and Emotional Well-being

Physical activity has been shown to improve mood and reduce symptoms of depression and anxiety. For seniors, maintaining a routine that includes exercise can provide a sense of purpose and accomplishment, enhancing overall well-being. The ketogenic diet, by stabilizing energy levels and potentially enhancing sleep quality, complements the mood-stabilizing effects of exercise.

7. Social Interaction and Community

Joining exercise groups or attending fitness classes can provide valuable social interaction, essential for mental health. For seniors on a ketogenic diet, being part of a community with similar health goals can provide support and motivation, making it easier to adhere to dietary and exercise plans.

Incorporating a routine that balances cardiovascular and strength-training exercises will maximize the benefits of the ketogenic diet for seniors, helping them lead healthier and more active lives. Seniors should consult healthcare providers to tailor exercise routines to their health conditions and physical capabilities, ensuring safe and effective physical activity.

Safe Exercise Practices for Older Adults

Integrating exercise into daily life is essential for seniors, especially those on a ketogenic diet. Still, it's crucial to approach physical activity with safety in mind to avoid injuries and ensure health benefits. This subchapter offers guidelines on safe exercise practices explicitly tailored for older adults, helping them maintain physical activity without risking their health.

1. Start with a Medical Check-Up

Before beginning any new exercise regimen, seniors should consult with a healthcare provider. This step is crucial to assessing their overall health, identifying risk factors, and receiving personalized advice based on their medical history and current health status.

2. Incorporate a Warm-Up and Cool-Down

Warming up before exercise and cooling down afterward is vital to prevent injuries. A warm-up should gently prepare the body for physical activity by gradually increasing the heart rate and loosening the joints and muscles. Cooling down helps to gradually reduce the heart rate and stretch the muscles, aiding in recovery and preventing stiffness.

3. Focus on Low-Impact Exercises

Low-impact exercises are generally safer and more suitable for seniors as they put less strain on the body, reducing the risk of joint and muscle injuries. Walking, swimming, cycling, and tai chi are excellent low-impact options that benefit cardiovascular health and muscle strength.

4. Use Proper Equipment

Using the correct equipment, such as supportive footwear, appropriate clothing, and safety gear (like helmets for biking), can significantly reduce the risk of falls and injuries. It's also essential to use any exercise equipment correctly and ensure it's adjusted to fit the senior's size and strength capabilities.

5. Stay Hydrated

Seniors are more prone to dehydration, which can be exacerbated by exercise, especially for those on a ketogenic diet. Drinking adequate fluids before, during, and after exercise is essential to prevent dehydration and maintain overall health.

6. Listen to Your Body

Seniors should be encouraged to listen to their bodies and recognize the signs of overexertion, such as excessive fatigue, dizziness, or pain. Pushing the body too hard can lead to injuries and setbacks in overall health. It's important to stop exercising immediately if any unusual or severe symptoms occur and to consult a healthcare provider if necessary.

7. Gradual Progression

Seniors need to start slowly with exercise and gradually increase the intensity and duration of their activities. This approach helps build endurance and strength safely over time, reducing the risk of injuries.

8. Regularly Update Exercise Plans

As seniors progress in their fitness journeys or their health conditions change, their exercise plans should be updated accordingly. Regular consultations with fitness professionals or healthcare providers can ensure that the exercise regimen remains appropriate and beneficial.

9. Incorporate Strength Training and Balance Exercises

Strength training is essential for maintaining muscle mass, which declines with age. Balance exercises, such as standing on one foot or practicing yoga, can help prevent falls by improving coordination and balance. Both types of exercise are crucial for seniors and should be included in a comprehensive exercise plan.

Strength training and balance exercises are essential for seniors to maintain muscle mass, bone density, and stability, all of which can help prevent falls and improve overall health. Here are some examples of both types of exercises that are well-suited for seniors:

Strength Training Exercises

1. **Chair Squats**
   - Stand in front of a chair with feet hip-width apart.
   - Slowly lower down as if to sit, bending the knees while keeping the back straight.
   - Touch the chair lightly, then stand back up.
   - Repeat 10-15 times.

2. **Wall Push-Ups**
   - Stand an arm's length in front of a wall.
   - Place palms flat Against the wall at shoulder height.
   - Bend elbows to bring your body towards the wall, keeping your feet flat.
   - Push back to the starting position.
   - Repeat 10-15 times.

3. **Bicep Curls with Light Weights**
   - Sit or stand with a lightweight in each hand, arms at your sides.
   - Curl the weights toward your shoulders, keeping elbows close to your body.
   - Lower the weights slowly back to the starting position.
   - Repeat 10-15 times.

4. **Seated Leg Lifts**
   - Sit in a sturdy chair with feet flat on the ground.
   - Straighten one leg out before you, hold for a few seconds, then lower it back down.
   - Repeat 10-15 times with each leg.

Balance Exercises

1. **Single-Leg Stand**
   - Stand behind a chair and hold on for balance.
   - Lift one leg off the floor and hold the position for up to 30 seconds.
   - Switch legs and repeat.
   - As balance improves, try performing without holding onto the chair.

2. **Heel-To-Toe Walk**
   - Position the heel of one foot just in front of the toes of the opposite foot each time you take a step.
   - Your heel and toes should touch or almost touch.
   - Walk 20 steps in a straight line, focusing on maintaining balance.

3. **Side Leg Raises**
   - Stand behind a chair and hold on for balance.
   - Lift one leg to the side, keep your back straight and your toes facing forward.
   - Hold for a few seconds, then lower the leg back to the starting position.
   - Repeat 10-15 times with each leg.

4. **Back Leg Raises**
   - Stand behind a chair and hold on for balance.
   - Slowly lift one leg straight back without bending the knees or pointing the toes.
   - Hold the position for a few seconds, then lower the leg.
   - Repeat 10-15 times with each leg.

These exercises are generally safe for most seniors. Still, it's always a good idea to consult with a healthcare provider before starting a new exercise program, mainly if pre-existing health conditions exist. By regularly performing these strength and balance exercises, seniors can enhance their physical stability and reduce the risk of falls, significantly improving their quality of life as they age.

By adhering to these safe exercise practices, seniors on a ketogenic diet can enjoy the physical and mental health benefits of regular physical activity while minimizing the risk of injury and other health issues.

28-Day Customized Exercise Plans: Women, Men, General Senior Plan

You will find these planners in the Bonus Section at the end of the Book.

Chapter 6: Morning Meals: Keto Breakfast Recipes (20 Recipes)

1: Ham and Cheese Egg Cups

Yields: 2 servings.

Time: A total of 25 minutes, of which 5 for preparation.

Calories per serving: 166 Kcal.

Ingredients:

- Butter/Oil/Cooking spray for frying pans (to grease the 2 muffin stamps)
- 2 pieces of ham
- One cup of cheddar, shredded (100 gr. Or 3.5 oz)
- two big eggs
- salt (1 gr or 0.04 oz)
- freshly ground black pepper (1 gr or 0.04 oz)
- freshly chopped parsley as a garnish

Step-by-step instructions:

Step 1: Grease 2 muffin cups (or small cooking cups) with cooking spray and preheat the oven to 400o. Place a ham slice in the middle of each cup, then top with cheddar cheese. Add salt and pepper to each ham cup before cracking an egg.

Step 2: Bake the eggs for 12 to 15 minutes or until cooked through, depending on your preference for runny yolks.

Step 3: Add parsley as a garnish and serve.

2. Breakfast Deviled Eggs

Yields: 2 to 3 servings (12 deviled eggs).
Time: 20 to 30 minutes, including 10/20 minutes of cooking time.
Calories: 277 per serving.

Ingredients:

- 6 large eggs
- 4 ounces (or 110 gr) full-fat cream cheese, softened at room temperature for 1 hour or more
- 1/4 teaspoon salt (1 gr or 0.04 oz)
- 1/2 teaspoon ground black pepper (1 gr or 0.04 oz)
- 1 tablespoon of everything bagel seasoning (10 gr or 0.4 oz)

Instructions:

Step 1: Boil the eggs hard. The simplest method is to cover the eggs with cold water, boil them, then take them off the heat and let them stand for eight to ten minutes. Once the eggs are drained, cool them in an ice bath.

Step 2: Cut them off. Cut the eggs in half lengthwise, then remove the yolks with a small spoon and transfer to a bowl.

Step 3: Roughly chop the cream cheese and mix it into the yolks. To make the mixture frothy and whipped, use a hand mixer or stick blender, blending at low and then at high speed. Stir in the pepper and salt. Smell. Taste and adjust spices.

Step 4: Spoon the yolk mixture into the egg whites using a spoon or piping bag. It will be quite stiff; if needed, microwave in brief bursts of two to three seconds to further soften.

Step 5: Season the tops of the filled eggs with a good amount of everything bagel spice. Serve right away.

3. Coconut Almond Porridge

Yields: 2 servings.

Time: 15 minutes.

Calories per serving: 280 Kcal.

Ingredients:
- 1/4 cup coconut flour (30 gr or 1 oz)
- 1/4 cup ground almonds (30 gr or 1 oz)
- 1 cup coconut milk (240 ml)
- 1 tablespoon erythritol (or another keto-friendly sweetener)
- 1/2 teaspoon vanilla extract
- Pinch of salt
- Cinnamon for sprinkling

Instructions:

Step 1: Combine coconut flour, ground almonds, and coconut milk in a small pot. Stir well to combine.

Step 2: Cook over medium heat, stirring constantly to prevent clumping, until the mixture thickens.

Step 3: Add erythritol, vanilla extract, and a pinch of salt. Cook for another 2-3 minutes until it reaches a porridge-like consistency.

Step 4: Divide the porridge into bowls, sprinkle with cinnamon, and serve warm.

4. Keto Avocado Smoothie

Yields: 2 servings.

Time: 10 minutes.

Calories per serving: 240 Kcal.

Ingredients:

- 1 large avocado
- 1 cup unsweet almond milk (240 ml)
- 1/4 cup heavy cream (60 ml)
- 1 tablespoon lemon juice
- 2 tablespoons erythritol
- Ice cubes
- Fresh mint for garnish

Instructions:

Step 1: Combine avocado, almond milk, heavy cream, lemon juice, erythritol, and ice cubes in a blender.

Step 2: Blend until smooth.

Step 3: Pour into glasses, garnish with fresh mint, and serve immediately.

5. Bacon and Spinach Frittata

Yields: 2 servings.

Time: 25 minutes.

Calories per serving: 320 Kcal.

Ingredients:

- 4 large eggs
- 4 slices of bacon, chopped
- 1 cup fresh spinach (30 gr or 1 oz)
- 1/4 cup shredded cheddar cheese (25 gr or 0.88 oz)
- Salt and pepper to taste
- 1 tablespoon olive oil

Instructions:

Step 1: Preheat the oven to 350°F (175°C).

Step 2: Cook bacon in a skillet until crispy. Remove the bacon and set aside, leaving the fat in the skillet.

Step 3: Add fresh spinach to the skillet and sauté until wilted.

Step 4: In a bowl, whisk together eggs, cooked bacon, sautéed spinach, cheddar cheese, salt, and pepper.

Step 5: Heat olive oil in a 10-inch oven-safe skillet over medium heat. Pour the egg mixture into the skillet and cook for 2-3 minutes until the edges begin to set.

Step 6: Transfer the skillet to the oven and bake for 12-15 minutes or until the frittata is set.

Step 7: Remove from oven, let cool slightly, and serve.

6. Smoked Salmon and Cream Cheese Roll-Ups

Yields: 2 servings.

Time: 10 minutes.

Calories per serving: 220 Kcal.

Ingredients:

- 4 oz smoked salmon (113 gr)
- 2 oz cream cheese, softened (56 gr)
- 1 tablespoon capers
- 1/4 red onion, thinly sliced
- Fresh dill for garnish

Instructions:

Step 1: Spread cream cheese evenly over slices of smoked salmon.

Step 2: Sprinkle capers and red onion over the cream cheese.

Step 3: Carefully roll up the smoked salmon slices.

Step 4: Garnish with fresh dill and serve.

7. Greek Yogurt Keto Parfait

Yields: 2 servings.

Time: 10 minutes.

Calories per serving: 200 Kcal.

Ingredients:

- 1 cup full-fat Greek yogurt (245 gr)
- 1/4 cup crushed walnuts (30 gr)
- 2 tablespoons sugar-free raspberry jam and red currant berries
- 1 tablespoon chia seeds

Instructions:

Step 1: In serving glasses, layer half of the Greek yogurt.

Step 2: Add a layer of sugar-free raspberry jam and red (or black) currant over the yogurt.

Step 3: Sprinkle a layer of crushed walnuts and chia seeds.

Step 4: Repeat the layers with the remaining ingredients.

Step 5: Serve immediately or chill in the refrigerator for 30 minutes before serving.

8. Keto Cream Cheese Pancakes

Yields: about 6 pancakes.

Time: 10 to 15 min.

Calories: 329.

Ingredients

- 4 ounces (100 gr) cream cheese at room temperature

- 2 large eggs

- 1/4 cup flour (30 gr or 1.06 oz), such as almond, coconut, or all-purpose

- 1/2 teaspoon (2.4 gr or 0.1 oz) baking powder

- 1/4 teaspoon fine salt (1 gr or 0.04 oz)

- Cooking spray or butter for greasing the pan

- Sliced strawberries and powdered sugar, or maple syrup, for serving

Instructions

Step 1: Place the cream cheese, eggs, flour, baking powder, and salt in a blender and blend until smooth.

Step 2: Heat a large nonstick frying pan over medium heat. Coat with cooking spray or butter. Once the butter is melted, pour 2 to 3 tablespoons of the batter. Cook until deep golden-brown is on the bottom for about 3 minutes. Flip and cook until the second side is golden-brown, 1 to 2 minutes more. Transfer to a plate.

Step 3: Repeat with the remaining batter. Serve with sliced strawberries, powdered sugar, or a drizzle of maple syrup.

9. Almond Flour Pancakes

Yields: 2 servings.

Time: 15 minutes.

Calories per serving: 265 Kcal.

Ingredients:

- 1 cup almond flour (96 gr or 3.4 oz)
- 2 large eggs
- 1/4 cup unsweetened almond milk (60 ml)
- 1 tablespoon granulated erythritol
- 1 teaspoon baking powder
- 1/2 teaspoon vanilla extract
- Butter or oil for cooking

Instructions:

Step 1: In a mixing bowl, combine almond flour, baking powder, and erythritol.

Step 2: In another bowl, whisk together eggs, almond milk, and vanilla extract.

Step 3: Mix the wet and dry ingredients until a batter forms.

Step 4: Heat a non-stick skillet over medium heat and grease lightly with butter or oil.

Step 5: Pour small amounts of batter onto the skillet. Cook for 2-3 minutes on each side or until golden brown.

Step 6: Serve hot with a pat of butter or a drizzle of sugar-free syrup.

10. Keto Breakfast Hash

Yields: 2 servings.

Time: 30 minutes.

Calories per serving: 350 Kcal.

Ingredients:

- 1 medium cauliflower head, riced (about 500 gr or 17.6 oz)
- 4 slices bacon, chopped
- 1/2 bell pepper, diced
- 1/4 onion, diced
- 2 cloves garlic, minced
- 2 tablespoons olive oil
- Salt and pepper to taste
- Fresh parsley for garnish

Instructions:

Step 1: Heat olive oil over medium heat in a large skillet. Add the bacon and cook until crisp.

Step 2: Add onion, bell pepper, and garlic to the skillet with the bacon and sauté until the vegetables are soft.

Step 3: Stir in the riced cauliflower, season with salt and pepper, and cook for about 10 minutes or until tender and slightly crispy.

Step 4: Garnish with fresh parsley before serving. Traditionally served with a fried egg on top or even better put the egg/s (1 or 2) in step 1.

11. Avocado and Egg Salad

Yields: 2 servings.

Time: 10 minutes.

Calories per serving: 300 Kcal.

Ingredients:

- 2 large hard-boiled eggs, peeled and chopped
- 1 large avocado, peeled and diced
- Small broccoli heads (100 gr or 3.5 oz), cooked and cut in smaller heads
- 2 tablespoons mayonnaise
- 1 teaspoon Dijon mustard
- Salt and pepper to taste
- Lemon juice to taste

Instructions:

Step 1: In a bowl, combine the chopped eggs, diced avocado, cooked broccoli heads, mayonnaise, and Dijon mustard.

Step 2: Season with salt, pepper, and a squeeze of lemon juice.

Step 3: Mix gently until well combined.

Step 4: Serve chilled, garnished with additional black pepper or herbs if desired.

12. Chia Pudding with Berries

Yields: 2 servings.

Time: 15 minutes (plus chilling time).

Calories per serving: 215 Kcal.

Ingredients:

- 1/4 cup chia seeds (40 gr or 1.4 oz)
- 1 cup unsweetened coconut milk (240 ml)
- 1 tablespoon granulated erythritol
- 1/2 teaspoon vanilla extract
- 1/4 cup mixed berries (blueberries, raspberries) (about 37 gr or 1.3 oz)

Instructions:

Step 1: In a bowl, combine chia seeds, coconut milk, erythritol, and vanilla extract.

Step 2: Stir well and let sit for 10 minutes, then stir again to prevent clumping.

Step 3: Cover and refrigerate for at least 2 hours or overnight until it thickens into a pudding-like consistency.

Step 4: Serve topped with mixed berries.

13. Keto Bulletproof Coffee

Yields: 1 serving.

Time: 5 minutes.

Calories per serving: 220 Kcal.

Ingredients:

- 1 cup of brewed coffee (240 ml)
- 1 tablespoon unsalted butter
- 1 tablespoon coconut oil or MCT oil
- Optional: a dash of cinnamon or vanilla extract for flavor

Instructions:

Step 1: Brew a fresh cup of coffee.

Step 2: Combine hot coffee, butter, and coconut oil (or MCT oil) in a blender.

Step 3: Blend on high for about 30 seconds until the mixture is smooth and creamy.

Step 4: Pour into a cup, add optional cinnamon or vanilla, and serve immediately.

14. Keto Ham and Cheese Muffins

Yields: 4 servings.

Time: 30 minutes.

Calories per serving: 300 Kcal.

Ingredients:
- 6 large eggs
- 1 cup diced ham
- 1/2 cup shredded cheddar cheese
- 1/4 cup finely chopped green onions
- Salt and pepper to taste
- Butter or oil for greasing muffin tins

Instructions:

Step 1: Preheat the oven to 350°F (175°C) and grease a muffin tin.

Step 2: In a large bowl, whisk the eggs. Add ham, cheese, green onions, salt, and pepper.

Step 3: Pour the egg mixture evenly into the muffin tins.

Step 4: Bake for 20-25 minutes or until the muffins are set and golden on top.

Step 5: Allow to cool slightly before serving.

15. Keto Avocado Bacon Boats

Yields: 2 servings.

Time: 15 minutes.

Calories per serving: 350 Kcal.

Ingredients:

- 2 avocados, halved and pitted
- 4 slices of bacon, cooked and crumbled
- 1/2 cup cherry tomatoes, halved
- Salt and pepper to taste
- Fresh cilantro for garnish

Instructions:

Step 1: Scoop out some of the avocado flesh to create a larger cavity.

Step 2: Fill each avocado half with crumbled bacon and cherry tomatoes.

Step 3: Season with salt and pepper.

Step 4: Garnish with fresh cilantro and serve.

16. Creamy Keto Porridge

Yields: 2 servings.

Time: 10 minutes.

Calories per serving: 250 Kcal.

Ingredients:

- 1/4 cup almond flour
- 2 tablespoons coconut flour
- 1 cup almond milk
- 1 tablespoon erythritol
- 1/2 teaspoon cinnamon
- 1 tablespoon butter

Instructions:

Step 1: In a small saucepan, mix almond flour and coconut flour with almond milk, stirring constantly to prevent clumps.

Step 2: Cook over medium heat until the mixture starts to thicken.

Step 3: Stir in erythritol, cinnamon, and butter until well combined and creamy.

Step 4: Serve hot with an optional sprinkle of cinnamon on top.

17. Keto Lemon Ricotta Pancakes

Yields: 2 servings.

Time: 20 minutes.

Calories per serving: 280 Kcal.

Ingredients:

- 1/2 cup almond flour (50 gr or 1.76 oz)
- 1/4 cup ricotta cheese (62 gr or 2.2 oz)
- 2 large eggs
- 1 tablespoon erythritol
- Zest of 1 lemon
- 1/2 teaspoon baking powder
- 1/4 teaspoon vanilla extract
- Butter or oil for cooking

Instructions:

Step 1: In a large bowl, whisk together eggs, ricotta cheese, lemon zest, and vanilla extract until smooth.

Step 2: Add almond flour, erythritol, and baking powder to the mixture and stir until well combined.

Step 3: Heat a skillet over medium heat and grease lightly with butter or oil.

Step 4: Scoop 1/4 cup of batter for each pancake onto the skillet. Cook for 2-3 minutes on each side or until golden brown.

Step 5: Serve hot with a pat of butter or a drizzle of sugar-free syrup.

18. Keto Vegetable Frittata

Yields: 4 servings.

Time: 35 minutes.

Calories per serving: 220 Kcal.

Ingredients:

- 6 large eggs
- 1/2 cup heavy cream (120 ml)
- 1 cup chopped spinach (30 gr or 1 oz)
- 1/2 cup diced bell peppers (75 gr or 2.6 oz)
- 1/4 cup chopped onions (40 gr or 1.4 oz)
- 1/2 cup grated cheddar cheese (50 gr or 1.8 oz)
- 2 tablespoons olive oil
- Salt and pepper to taste

Instructions:

Step 1: Preheat the oven to 375°F (190°C).

Step 2: In a bowl, whisk together eggs, heavy cream, salt, and pepper.

Step 3: Heat olive oil in an oven-safe skillet over medium heat. Sauté onions and bell peppers until softened.

Step 4: Add spinach and cook until wilted.

Step 5: Pour the egg mixture over the vegetables in the skillet. Sprinkle with cheddar cheese.

Step 6: Transfer the skillet to the oven and bake for 20 minutes or until the frittata is set. Step 7: Remove from oven, let cool slightly, and serve.

19. Keto Blueberry Muffins

Yields: 6 muffins. 2/3 servings.

Time: 30 minutes.

Calories per serving: 180 Kcal.

Ingredients:

- 1 cup almond flour (96 gr or 3.4 oz)
- 1/3 cup erythritol (70 gr or 2.5 oz)
- 2 large eggs
- 1/4 cup unsalted butter, melted (60 ml)
- 1/2 teaspoon baking powder
- 1/4 teaspoon salt
- 1/2 cup fresh blueberries (75 gr or 2.6 oz)
- 1 teaspoon vanilla extract

Instructions:

Step 1: Preheat the oven to 350°F (175°C) and line a muffin tin with paper liners.

Step 2: In a large bowl, mix almond flour, erythritol, baking powder, and salt.

Step 3: In another bowl, whisk together eggs, melted butter, and vanilla extract.

Step 4: Combine wet and dry ingredients until well-mixed. Fold in blueberries gently.

Step 5: Divide the batter evenly among the muffin cups.

Step 6: Bake for 20-25 minutes or until a toothpick inserted into the center comes out clean.

Step 7: Remove from oven, allow to cool for 10 minutes in the pan, then transfer to a wire rack to cool completely.

20. Keto Sausage and Egg Breakfast Skillet

Yields: 2 servings

Time: 25 minutes

Calories per serving: 400 Kcal

Ingredients:

- 4 large eggs
- 2 links of sugar-free pork sausage, sliced
- 1/2 cup diced red bell pepper (75 gr or 2.6 oz)
- 1/4 cup diced onion (40 gr or 1.4 oz)
- 1 cup fresh spinach (30 gr or 1 oz)
- 2 tablespoons olive oil
- Salt and pepper to taste

Instructions:

Step 1: Heat olive oil in a skillet over medium heat. Add sausage slices and cook until browned.

Step 2: Add onions and bell peppers to the skillet, sautéing until softened.

Step 3: Add spinach and cook until wilted.

Step 4: Crack eggs over the sausage and vegetable mixture. Cover and cook for 5-7 minutes or until eggs are cooked to your liking.

Step 5: Season with salt and pepper and serve directly from the skillet.

Chapter 7: Midday Meals: Keto Lunch Recipes (25 recipes)

1. Greek bouyiourdi

Yields: 4 servings

Time: 40 min of which 30 min cooking time

Calories per serving: 243

Ingredients

- 3 large ripe tomatoes
- 1 garlic clove, crushed
- 200g block feta (or 8 oz)
- 1 large mild green chilli or 1 green pepper, sliced
- 1 tsp roughly chopped oregano leaves
- 4 tbsp olive oil
- warmed pitta bread or keto bread to serve

Instructions

Step 1: Cut 1 tomato through the middle, then cut two slices from the center and set aside. Scoop the seeds from the rest of the tomato, then grate the flesh, discarding the skin. Deseed and grate the rest of the tomatoes similarly, then mix the grated flesh with the garlic. Season and spoon into a 16cm baking dish.

Step 2: Heat the oven to 200C/180C fan/gas 6. Nestle the feta block in the garlicky tomatoes, then top with the sliced tomatoes, the chilli, oregano, olive oil and a pinch of sea salt. Cover the dish and bake for 15 mins, then uncover and bake for a further 15 mins. Serve warm with the pitta or keto bread on the side for dunking.

2. Keto Chicken Salad with Avocado and Bacon

Yields: 2 servings

Time: 20 minutes

Calories per serving: 450 Kcal

Ingredients:

- 2 cups cooked chicken breast, diced (about 300 gr or 10.5 oz)

- 1 ripe avocado, diced

- 4 slices of bacon, cooked crisp and crumbled

- 1/4 cup mayonnaise (60 gr or 2.1 oz)

- 1 tablespoon Dijon mustard

- 1/4 red onion, finely chopped

- Salt and pepper to taste

- Fresh lettuce leaves for serving

Instructions:

Step 1: In a large mixing bowl, combine the diced chicken, diced avocado, crumbled bacon, and chopped red onion.

Step 2: In a small bowl, mix mayonnaise and Dijon mustard. Pour this dressing over the chicken mixture.

Step 3: Gently toss all ingredients until well combined—season with salt and pepper to taste.

Step 4: Chill for about 10 minutes before serving.

Step 5: Serve the chicken salad in fresh lettuce leaves as wrap

3. Keto Cauliflower Soup

Yields: 4 servings

Time: 30 minutes

Calories per serving: 180 Kcal

Ingredients:

- 1 medium head cauliflower, chopped into florets (about 500 gr or 17.6 oz)

- 2 tablespoons olive oil (30 ml)

- 1 medium onion, chopped

- 2 cloves garlic, minced

- 4 cups chicken or vegetable broth (960 ml)

- 1/2 cup heavy cream (120 ml)

- Salt and pepper to taste

- Chopped chives for garnish

Instructions:

Step 1: Heat olive oil in a large pot over medium heat. Add onion and garlic, sautéing until soft and translucent.

Step 2: Add cauliflower florets and continue to cook for about 5 minutes, stirring occasionally.

Step 3: Pour in the broth and bring to a boil. Reduce heat and let simmer for about 20 minutes or until the cauliflower is tender.

Step 4: Use an immersion blender to purée the soup until smooth.

Step 5: Stir in heavy cream and heat through. Season with salt and pepper.

Step 6: Serve hot, garnished with chopped chives

4. Keto Zucchini Noodle Salad

Yields: 2 servings

Time: 15 minutes

Calories per serving: 220 Kcal

Ingredients:

- 2 medium zucchinis, spiralized into noodles (about 500 gr or 17.6 oz)

- 1 cup cherry tomatoes, halved (about 150 gr or 5.3 oz)

- 1/2 cup feta cheese, crumbled (about 75 gr or 2.6 oz)

- 1/4 cup black olives, sliced (about 30 gr or 1 oz)

- 2 tablespoons olive oil (30 ml)

- 1 tablespoon lemon juice

- Salt and pepper to taste

- Fresh basil leaves, torn for garnish

Instructions:

Step 1: Place spiralized zucchini noodles in a large salad bowl.

Step 2: Add cherry tomatoes, crumbled feta cheese, and sliced olives to the bowl.

Step 3: Whisk together olive oil and lemon juice in a small bowl. Drizzle this dressing over the salad.

Step 4: Toss everything together until well-mixed. Season with salt and pepper.

Step 5: Garnish with fresh basil leaves before serving.

5. Keto Beef Stir-Fry

Yields: 2 servings

Time: 20 minutes

Calories per serving: 350 Kcal

Ingredients:

- 300 gr or 10.5 oz thinly sliced beef steak

- 1 bell pepper, sliced (about 150 gr or 5.3 oz)

- 1/2 onion, sliced (about 75 gr or 2.6 oz)

- 2 tablespoons coconut oil (30 ml)

- 2 tablespoons soy sauce (or tamari for gluten-free) (30 ml)

- 1 teaspoon sesame oil (5 ml)

- 1 clove garlic, minced

- 1 teaspoon ginger, grated

- Salt and pepper to taste

Instructions:

Step 1: Heat coconut oil in a large skillet over medium-high heat.

Step 2: Add beef slices to the skillet and stir-fry for about 3-5 minutes or until browned.

Step 3: Add sliced bell pepper, onion, garlic, and ginger to the skillet. Continue to stir-fry for another 5 minutes until vegetables are tender.

Step 4: Drizzle soy sauce and sesame oil over the stir-fry. Mix well to combine.

Step 5: Season with salt and pepper to taste.

Step 6: Serve hot, ideally over a bed of cauliflower rice, for a complete meal.

6. Keto Salmon Salad

Yields: 2 servings

Time: 20 minutes

Calories per serving: 400 Kcal

Ingredients:

- 2 salmon fillets (about 150 gr or 5 oz each)

- 1 tablespoon olive oil (15 ml)

- 4 cups mixed salad greens (about 120 gr or 4.2 oz)

- 1/4 cup diced cucumber (about 50 gr or 1.8 oz)

- 1/4 cup diced avocado (about 50 gr or 1.8 oz)

- 2 tablespoons mayonnaise (30 ml)

- 1 tablespoon lemon juice (15 ml)

- Salt and pepper to taste

- Fresh dill for garnish

Instructions:

Step 1: Heat olive oil in a pan over medium heat. Season salmon fillets with salt and pepper, and cook for about 4-5 minutes on each side or until cooked through.

Step 2: In a large bowl, mix salad greens, cucumber, and avocado.

Step 3: Combine mayonnaise and lemon juice in a small bowl to make a dressing.

Step 4: Flake the cooked salmon and add to the salad.

Step 5: Drizzle the dressing over the salad and toss gently.

Step 6: Garnish with fresh dill and serve immediately.

7. Keto Turkey and Avocado Wraps

Yields: 2 servings

Time: 15 minutes

Calories per serving: 400 Kcal

Ingredients:

- 200 gr or 7 oz sliced turkey breast

- 1 large avocado, sliced (about 200 gr or 7 oz)

- 1/2 cup arugula (about 15 gr or 0.5 oz)

- 2 tablespoons mayonnaise (30 gr or 1 oz)

- 4 large lettuce leaves

- Salt and pepper to taste

Instructions:

Step 1: Lay the lettuce leaves flat on a clean surface.

Step 2: Spread mayonnaise evenly over each lettuce leaf.

Step 3: Arrange turkey and avocado slices on the mayonnaise.

Step 4: Add a handful of arugula to each wrap.

Step 5: Season with salt and pepper.

Step 6: Carefully roll the lettuce leaves to enclose the fillings.

Step 7: Serve immediately or wrap in plastic for an on-the-go option.

8. Keto Creamy Mushroom Soup

Yields: 4 servings

Time: 30 minutes

Calories per serving: 250 Kcal

Ingredients:

- 300 gr or 10.5 oz mushrooms, sliced
- 1 small onion, diced (about 100 gr or 3.5 oz)
- 2 cloves garlic, minced
- 2 tablespoons unsalted butter (30 gr or 1 oz)
- 500 ml or 17 oz chicken or vegetable broth
- 120 ml or 4 oz heavy cream
- Salt and pepper to taste
- Fresh parsley, chopped for garnish

Instructions:

Step 1: Melt butter in a large pot over medium heat.

Step 2: Add onion and garlic, and sauté until translucent.

Step 3: Add mushrooms and cook until they are soft and browned.

Step 4: Pour in broth and bring to a simmer. Cook for 20 minutes.

Step 5: Blend the soup using an immersion blender until smooth.

Step 6: Stir in heavy cream and season with salt and pepper.

Step 7: Heat through, but do not boil.

Step 8: Serve hot, garnished with chopped parsley.

9. Keto Tuna Salad Stuffed Tomatoes

Yields: 2 servings

Time: 20 minutes

Calories per serving: 300 Kcal

Ingredients:

- 4 large tomatoes (about 800 gr or 28 oz total)

- 1 can tuna in oil, drained (about 140 gr or 5 oz)

- 1/4 cup mayonnaise (60 gr or 2 oz)

- 1/4 red onion, finely chopped (about 30 gr or 1 oz)

- 1 celery stalk, finely chopped (about 30 gr or 1 oz)

- Salt and pepper to taste

- Fresh herbs like dill or parsley, chopped for garnish

Instructions:

Step 1: Cut the tops off the tomatoes and hollow out the insides using a spoon.

Step 2: In a bowl, mix tuna, mayonnaise, chopped onion, and celery.

Step 3: Season the tuna mixture with salt and pepper.

Step 4: Spoon the tuna salad into the hollowed-out tomatoes.

Step 5: Garnish with fresh herbs and serve chilled.

10. Keto Chicken Caesar Salad

Yields: 2 servings

Time: 20 minutes

Calories per serving: 450 Kcal

Ingredients:

- 2 cups cooked chicken breast, chopped (about 300 gr or 10.5 oz)

- 4 cups romaine lettuce, chopped (about 200 gr or 7 oz)

- 1/2 cup Parmesan cheese, shredded (about 50 gr or 1.8 oz)

- 1/4 cup Caesar dressing (60 ml or 2 oz)

- 2 tablespoons bacon bits (30 gr or 1 oz)

- Salt and pepper to taste

Instructions:

Step 1: Combine chopped romaine lettuce and cooked chicken breast in a large salad bowl.

Step 2: Add Caesar dressing and toss to coat evenly.

Step 3: Sprinkle shredded Parmesan cheese and bacon bits over the top.

Step 4: Season with salt and pepper.

Step 5: Toss lightly and serve immediately.

11. Keto Shrimp and Avocado Salad

Yields: 2 servings

Time: 15 minutes

Calories per serving: 350 Kcal

Ingredients:

- 200 gr or 7 oz cooked shrimp, peeled and deveined

- 1 large avocado, diced (about 200 gr or 7 oz)

- 1/2 cucumber, diced (about 100 gr or 3.5 oz)

- 1/4 cup lime juice (60 ml or 2 oz)

- 2 tablespoons olive oil (30 ml or 1 oz)

- Salt and pepper to taste

- Fresh cilantro, chopped for garnish

Instructions:

Step 1: In a mixing bowl, combine cooked shrimp, diced avocado, and diced cucumber.

Step 2: Whisk together lime juice and olive oil in a small bowl.

Step 3: Pour the dressing over the shrimp and avocado mixture.

Step 4: Season with salt and pepper and toss gently to combine.

Step 5: Garnish with chopped cilantro and serve immediately.

12. Keto Cobb Salad

Yields: 2 servings

Time: 20 minutes

Calories per serving: 400 Kcal

Ingredients:

- 2 cups chopped romaine lettuce (about 150 gr or 5.3 oz)
- 1 medium avocado, diced (about 150 gr or 5.3 oz)
- 100 gr or 3.5 oz cooked chicken breast, diced
- 2 hard-boiled eggs, sliced
- 100 gr or 3.5 oz bacon, cooked and crumbled
- 50 gr or 1.8 oz blue cheese, crumbled
- 10 cherry tomatoes, halved (about 100 gr or 3.5 oz)
- 2 tablespoons ranch dressing (30 ml or 1 oz)
- Salt and pepper to taste

Instructions:

Step 1: Arrange the chopped romaine lettuce in a large serving bowl.

Step 2: Neatly place diced avocado, chicken, sliced eggs, crumbled bacon, blue cheese, and halved cherry tomatoes on the lettuce.

Step 3: Drizzle with ranch dressing and season with salt and pepper.

Step 4: Toss gently before serving or serve as is for a layered presentation.

13. Keto Salmon Spinach Salad

Yields: 2 servings

Time: 15 minutes

Calories per serving: 450 Kcal

Ingredients:

- 2 salmon fillets (150 gr or 5.3 oz each)
- 200 gr or 7 oz fresh spinach leaves
- 1/2 red onion, thinly sliced (about 50 gr or 1.8 oz)
- 1 tablespoon olive oil (15 ml)
- 2 tablespoons lemon juice (30 ml)
- Salt and pepper to taste
- 1 tablespoon capers (15 gr or 0.5 oz)

Instructions:

Step 1: Grill the salmon fillets over medium heat for about 5-6 minutes on each side or until cooked through.

Step 2: Arrange fresh spinach leaves on plates.

Step 3: Place grilled salmon on top of the spinach.

Step 4: Scatter sliced red onion and capers over the salmon.

Step 5: Whisk olive oil and lemon juice together and drizzle over the salad.

Step 6: Season with salt and pepper and serve immediately.

14. Keto Stuffed Bell Peppers

Yields: 4 servings

Time: 45 minutes

Calories per serving: 350 Kcal

Ingredients:

- 4 bell peppers, tops cut off and seeds removed (about 800 gr or 28 oz total)
- 400 gr or 14 oz ground beef
- 1/4 cup chopped onion (about 40 gr or 1.4 oz)
- 1 clove garlic, minced
- 1 cup cauliflower rice (about 100 gr or 3.5 oz)
- 100 gr or 3.5 oz shredded cheddar cheese
- 2 tablespoons olive oil (30 ml)
- Salt and pepper to taste

Instructions:

Step 1: Preheat oven to 375°F (190°C).

Step 2: Heat olive oil in a skillet over medium heat. Add ground beef, onion, and garlic. Cook until beef is browned.

Step 3: Stir in cauliflower rice and cook for another 5 minutes.

Step 4: Spoon the beef and cauliflower mixture into hollowed-out bell peppers.

Step 5: Top each pepper with shredded cheddar cheese.

Step 6: Place stuffed peppers in a baking dish and bake for 30 minutes.

Step 7: Serve hot, seasoned with salt and pepper.

15. Keto Turkey Lettuce Wraps

Yields: 2 servings

Time: 15 minutes

Calories per serving: 300 Kcal

Ingredients:

- 200 gr or 7 oz ground turkey
- 1 tablespoon sesame oil (15 ml)
- 1 clove garlic, minced
- 1 teaspoon grated ginger
- 1 tablespoon soy sauce (15 ml)
- 6 large lettuce leaves (about 100 gr or 3.5 oz)
- 1/4 cup sliced green onions (about 25 gr or 0.9 oz)
- 1 tablespoon hoisin sauce (15 ml)
- Fresh cilantro for garnish

Instructions:

Step 1: Heat sesame oil in a skillet over medium heat. Add ground turkey, garlic, and ginger. Cook until turkey is browned.

Step 2: Stir in soy sauce and hoisin sauce, and cook for an additional 5 minutes.

Step 3: Spoon the turkey mixture into lettuce leaves.

Step 4: Top with sliced green onions and fresh cilantro.

Step 5: Serve immediately as wraps.

16. Keto Cream of Broccoli Soup

Yields: 4 servings

Time: 30 minutes

Calories per serving: 250 Kcal

Ingredients:

- 500 gr or 17.6 oz broccoli, chopped
- 1 medium onion, chopped (about 100 gr or 3.5 oz)
- 2 cloves garlic, minced
- 3 cups vegetable broth (720 ml)
- 1 cup heavy cream (240 ml)
- 2 tablespoons butter (30 gr or 1 oz)
- Salt and pepper to taste

Instructions:

Step 1: Melt butter in a large pot over medium heat. Add onion and garlic, and sauté until translucent.

Step 2: Add chopped broccoli and vegetable broth and bring to a boil. Reduce heat and simmer until broccoli is tender, about 15-20 minutes.

Step 3: Use an immersion blender to puree the soup until smooth.

Step 4: Stir in heavy cream and heat through, careful not to boil.

Step 5: Season with salt and pepper.

Step 6: Serve hot, garnished with extra cream if desired.

17. Keto Lemon Herb Grilled Chicken

Yields: 2 servings

Time: 30 minutes (including marinating time)

Calories per serving: 320 Kcal

Ingredients:

- 2 chicken breasts (about 400 gr or 14 oz total)
- 2 tablespoons olive oil (30 ml)
- Juice of 1 lemon (about 2 tablespoons or 30 ml)
- 1 teaspoon dried herbs (basil, oregano, thyme) (5 gr)
- 2 cloves garlic, minced
- Salt and pepper to taste

Instructions:

Step 1: In a bowl, whisk together olive oil, lemon juice, dried herbs, minced garlic, salt, and pepper.

Step 2: Place the chicken breasts in a sealable plastic bag and pour the marinade over them. Seal the bag and marinate in the refrigerator for at least 20 minutes.

Step 3: Preheat the grill to medium-high heat. Remove the chicken from the marinade and grill for about 6-7 minutes on each side or until it is fully cooked and has nice grill marks.

Step 4: Let the chicken rest for a few minutes before slicing.

Step 5: Serve with a side of mixed greens or keto-friendly vegetables.

18. Keto Avocado Bacon Salad

Yields: 2 servings

Time: 15 minutes

Calories per serving: 400 Kcal

Ingredients:
- 100 gr or 3.5 oz cooked Bacon
- 1 large avocado, diced (about 150 gr or 5.3 oz)
- 100 gr or 3.5 oz mixed greens
- 1/2 cup cherry tomatoes, halved (about 75 gr or 2.6 oz)
- 1/4 red onion, thinly sliced (about 30 gr or 1 oz)
- 2 tablespoons extra virgin olive oil (30 ml)
- 1 tablespoon apple cider vinegar (15 ml)
- Salt and pepper to taste
- Fresh cilantro, chopped (for garnish)

Instructions:

Step 1: In a large salad bowl, combine cooked bacon, diced avocado, mixed greens, halved cherry tomatoes, and sliced red onion.

Step 2: In a small bowl, whisk together olive oil, apple cider vinegar, salt, and pepper to create a dressing.

Step 3: Drizzle the dressing over the salad and toss gently to coat.

Step 4: Garnish with chopped cilantro and serve immediately.

19. Keto Smoked Salmon Platter

Yields: 2 servings

Time: 10 minutes

Calories per serving: 310 Kcal

Ingredients:

- 200 gr or 7 oz smoked salmon
- 100 gr or 3.5 oz cream cheese
- 1 medium cucumber, sliced (about 150 gr or 5.3 oz)
- 2 tablespoons capers (30 gr or 1 oz)
- 1 small red onion, thinly sliced (about 50 gr or 1.8 oz)
- Fresh dill for garnish

Instructions:

Step 1: Arrange smoked salmon slices on a large plate.

Step 2: Place dollops of cream cheese sporadically over the salmon.

Step 3: Scatter sliced cucumber, capers, and red onion around and on the salmon.

Step 4: Garnish with fresh dill and serve as a refreshing, no-cook meal.

20. Keto Spinach and Feta Stuffed Chicken

Yields: 2 servings

Time: 35 minutes

Calories per serving: 420 Kcal

Ingredients:

- 2 chicken breasts (about 400 gr or 14 oz total)
- 150 gr or 5.3 oz fresh spinach, sautéed and drained
- 100 gr or 3.5 oz feta cheese, crumbled
- 2 tablespoons olive oil (30 ml)
- Salt and pepper to taste

Instructions:

Step 1: Preheat oven to 375°F (190°C).

Step 2: Cut a pocket into each chicken breast. Stuff with sautéed spinach and crumbled feta cheese.

Step 3: Secure the openings with toothpicks.

Step 4: Season the outside with salt and pepper, then heat olive oil in a pan and sear chicken on both sides until golden.

Step 5: Transfer to the oven and bake for 20 minutes or until chicken is cooked through. Step 6: Serve hot with a side of keto-friendly vegetables.

21. Keto Lemon Garlic Shrimp

Yields: 2 servings

Time: 20 minutes

Calories per serving: 350 Kcal

Ingredients:

- 300 gr or 10.5 oz shrimp, peeled and deveined
- 3 tablespoons olive oil (45 ml)
- Juice of 1 lemon (about 2 tablespoons or 30 ml)
- 3 cloves garlic, minced
- Salt and pepper to taste
- Fresh parsley, chopped for garnish

Instructions:

Step 1: Heat olive oil in a skillet over medium heat.

Step 2: Add minced garlic and sauté for 1 minute until fragrant.

Step 3: Add shrimp and cook for 5-7 minutes or until pink and cooked through.

Step 4: Pour lemon juice over shrimp, season with salt and pepper, and toss to coat evenly.

Step 5: Garnish with chopped parsley and serve hot with steamed asparagus or zucchini noodles.

22. Keto Balsamic Beef Pot Roast

Yields: 4 servings

Time: 6 hours (slow cooker method)

Calories per serving: 450 Kcal

Ingredients:

- 800 gr or 28 oz beef chuck roast
- 2 tablespoons olive oil (30 ml)
- 1 cup beef broth (240 ml)
- 1/4 cup balsamic vinegar (60 ml)
- 1 medium onion, sliced (100 gr or 3.5 oz)
- 3 cloves garlic, minced
- 1 teaspoon dried thyme (1 gr)
- Salt and pepper to taste

Instructions:

Step 1: Heat olive oil in a large skillet over medium-high heat. Brown the beef roast on all sides.

Step 2: Transfer the beef to a slow cooker. Add the sliced onion, minced garlic, and dried thyme.

Step 3: Pour beef broth and balsamic vinegar over the beef.

Step 4: Cook on low for 6 hours or until the beef is tender and pulls apart easily with a fork.

Step 5: Season with salt and pepper to taste.

Step 6: Serve hot, garnished with fresh herbs if desired.

23. Keto Salmon Nicoise Salad

Yields: 2 servings

Time: 30 minutes

Calories per serving: 380 Kcal

Ingredients:

- 300 gr or 10.5 oz fresh salmon fillet
- 100 gr or 3.5 oz green beans, trimmed
- 2 hard-boiled eggs, quartered
- 10 black olives, pitted (30 gr or 1 oz)
- 2 tablespoons capers (30 gr or 1 oz)
- 1 tablespoon olive oil (15 ml)
- 1 teaspoon Dijon mustard (5 ml)
- 1 tablespoon red wine vinegar (15 ml)
- Salt and pepper to taste
- Mixed salad greens (150 gr or 5.3 oz)

Instructions:

Step 1: Grill or pan-fry the salmon until cooked through and flaky.

Step 2: Blanch green beans in boiling water for 2-3 minutes, then plunge into ice water to stop cooking.

Step 3: To make the dressing, whisk together olive oil, Dijon mustard, red wine vinegar, salt, and pepper in a small bowl.

Step 4: Arrange mixed salad greens on plates. Top with cooked salmon, green beans, quartered eggs, olives, and capers.

Step 5: Drizzle the dressing over the salad.

Step 6: Serve immediately.

24. Keto Lemon-Herb Roasted Chicken Thighs

Yields: 4 servings

Time: 50 minutes

Calories per serving: 410 Kcal

Ingredients:

- 8 chicken thighs, bone-in and skin-on (about 1200 gr or 42 oz total)
- 2 tablespoons olive oil (30 ml)
- Juice and zest of 1 lemon (about 30 ml juice)
- 1 tablespoon fresh rosemary, chopped (1.5 gr)
- 1 tablespoon fresh thyme, chopped (1.5 gr)
- 3 cloves garlic, minced
- Salt and pepper to taste

Instructions:

Step 1: Preheat the oven to 375°F (190°C).

Step 2: In a small bowl, mix olive oil, lemon juice and zest, chopped rosemary, thyme, minced garlic, salt, and pepper.

Step 3: Rub the herb mixture all over the chicken thighs, ensuring it also gets under the skin.

Step 4: Place chicken thighs skin-side up in a roasting pan.

Step 5: Roast for 40-45 minutes or until the chicken is golden brown and cooked through. Step 6: Serve hot with a side of steamed or roasted vegetables.

25. Keto Creamy Tuscan Chicken

Yields: 2 servings

Time: 30 minutes

Calories per serving: 500 Kcal

Ingredients:

- 2 chicken breasts (about 400 gr or 14 oz total)
- 2 tablespoons olive oil (30 ml)
- 1/2 cup sun-dried tomatoes, chopped (90 gr or 3.2 oz)
- 2 cups fresh spinach (60 gr or 2.1 oz)
- 1/2 cup heavy cream (120 ml)
- 1/4 cup grated Parmesan cheese (30 gr or 1 oz)
- 3 cloves garlic, minced
- 1/2 cup chicken broth (120 ml)
- Salt and pepper to taste
- 1 teaspoon Italian seasoning (2 gr)

Instructions:

Step 1: Season chicken breasts with salt, pepper, and Italian seasoning.

Step 2: Heat olive oil in a large skillet over medium-high heat. Add chicken breasts and cook for about 5-7 minutes on each side until golden brown is cooked through. Remove chicken from the skillet and set aside.

Step 3: Add minced garlic and sun-dried tomatoes in the same skillet. Sauté for 1-2 minutes until garlic is fragrant.

Step 4: Pour in chicken broth and bring to a simmer, allowing the mixture to reduce slightly about 3-5 minutes.

Step 5: Lower the heat and stir in heavy cream and Parmesan cheese. Cook for another 2-3 minutes until the sauce thickens.

Step 6: Add spinach to the skillet, stirring until the spinach wilts.

Step 7: Return the chicken to the skillet and spoon the sauce over the chicken. Cook for an additional 2-3 minutes to reheat the chicken and blend the flavors.

Step 8: Serve hot, garnished with additional Parmesan if desired.

Chapter 8: Evening Meals: Keto Dinner Recipes

1. Keto Pesto Chicken Casserole

Yields: 4 servings

Time: 45 minutes

Calories per serving: 485 Kcal

Ingredients:

- 4 chicken breasts (approx. 800 gr or 28 oz total)
- 200 gr or 7 oz cream cheese
- 150 gr or 5.3 oz fresh spinach
- 100 gr or 3.5 oz homemade or store-bought pesto
- 50 gr or 1.8 oz sun-dried tomatoes, chopped
- 100 gr or 3.5 oz shredded mozzarella cheese
- Salt and pepper to taste

Instructions:

Step 1: Preheat your oven to 375°F (190°C).

Step 2: Lay out the chicken breasts in a baking dish and season with salt and pepper.

Step 3: In a bowl, mix the cream cheese, pesto, and sun-dried tomatoes until combined. Spread this mixture over the chicken.

Step 4: Scatter spinach over the top, then sprinkle mozzarella cheese.

Step 5: Bake in the oven for about 30 minutes, or until the chicken is cooked through and the cheese is bubbly and golden.

Step 6: Serve hot, garnished with additional pesto if desired.

2. Herb-crusted salmon with Creamy Dill Sauce

Yields: 4 servings

Time: 30\40 min of which 20 min cooking time

Calories: 380

Ingredients:

- Salmon fillets, 4 pieces (150g each, approximately 5 ounces each)
- Fresh dill, 30g (about 1 ounce)
- Fresh parsley, 30g (about 1 ounce)
- Almond flour, 50g (about 1.76 ounces)
- Olive oil, 30ml (about 1 fluid ounce)
- Garlic, minced, 10g (about 0.35 ounces)
- Full-fat Greek yogurt, 120g (about 4.23 ounces)
- Lemon juice, 20ml (about 0.7 fluid ounces)
- Salt and pepper to taste

Instructions:

Step 1: Preheat your oven to 200°C (400°F).

Step 2: Finely chop the dill and parsley and mix with almond flour, olive oil, minced garlic, salt, and pepper to create a crust.

Step 3: Place the salmon fillets on a baking sheet lined with parchment paper and press the herb mixture on top of each fillet.

Step 4: Bake for 12-15 minutes or until the salmon is cooked through and the crust is golden.

Step 5: For the sauce, mix Greek yogurt, dill, lemon juice, and a pinch of salt.

Step 6: Serve the salmon with a dollop of creamy dill sauce

3. Stuffed Bell Peppers with Ground Beef and Cauliflower Rice

Yields: 2 servings

Time: 45 min

Calories: 320

Ingredients:

- Large bell peppers, 4 pieces (approx 200g each, 7 ounces each)
- Ground beef, 450g (about 16 ounces)
- Cauliflower, riced, 300g (about 10.5 ounces)
- Onion, finely chopped, 50g (about 1.76 ounces)
- Chopped tomatoes, 150g (about 5.29 ounces)
- Shredded cheddar cheese, 100g (about 3.5 ounces)
- Olive oil, 20ml (about 0.68 fluid ounces)
- Cumin, 5g (about 0.18 ounces)
- Salt and pepper to taste

Instructions:

1. Preheat your oven to 175°C (350°F).
2. Halve the bell peppers lengthwise and remove the seeds.
3. In a skillet, heat olive oil over medium heat and sauté onions until translucent.
4. Add ground beef, cumin, salt, and pepper, cooking until the beef is browned.
5. Mix in riced cauliflower and chopped tomatoes, cooking for an additional 5 minutes.
6. Stuff the bell pepper halves with the beef and cauliflower mixture.
7. Top each half with shredded cheese.
8. Bake for 20-25 minutes or until the peppers are tender and the cheese is melted.

4. Keto Chicken Alfredo with Zucchini Noodles

Yields:

Time:

Calories:

Ingredients:

- Chicken breasts, 2 large (450g, about 16 ounces total)
- Zucchini, turned into noodles, 400g (about 14 ounces)
- Heavy cream, 100ml (about 3.4 fluid ounces)
- Parmesan cheese, grated, 50g (about 1.76 ounces)
- Butter, 30g (about 1 ounce)
- Garlic, minced, 10g (about 0.35 ounces)
- Salt and pepper to taste

Instructions:

Step 1: Season the Chicken breasts with salt and pepper.

Step 2: In a skillet, melt butter over medium heat and cook the chicken until golden and cooked through, about 6-7 minutes per side.

Step 3: Remove the chicken and set it aside. Add the minced garlic and sauté for 1 minute in the same skillet.

Step 4: Add heavy cream and bring to a simmer.

Step 5: Stir in Parmesan cheese until the sauce thickens.

Step 6: Add zucchini noodles to the skillet, tossing for 2-3 minutes to heat through.

Step 7: Slice the chicken and serve over the creamy zucchini noodles.

5. Keto Lamb Chops with Mint Pesto

Yields: 2 servings

Time: 15/20 min

Calories: 320

Ingredients:

- Lamb chops, 4 pieces (each 150g, about 5 ounces)
- Fresh mint, 50g (about 1.76 ounces)
- Almonds, crushed, 30g (about 1 ounce)
- Olive oil, 50ml (about 1.7 fluid ounces)
- Garlic, minced, 10g (about 0.35 ounces)
- Lemon zest, 5g (about 0.18 ounces)
- Salt and pepper to taste

Instructions:

Step 1: Preheat your grill to high heat.

Step 2: Season the lamb chops with salt and pepper.

Step 3: Grill the lamb chops to your preferred doneness, about 3-4 minutes per side for medium-rare.

Step 4: To make the mint pesto, blend the mint, crushed almonds, garlic, lemon zest, olive oil, and salt in a food processor until smooth.

Step 5: Serve the grilled lamb chops drizzled with mint pesto.

6. Keto Shrimp Scampi with Asparagus

Yields: 4

Time: 40

Calories: 350

Ingredients:
- Shrimp, peeled and deveined, 450g (about 16 ounces)
- Asparagus, trimmed, 250g (about 8.8 ounces)
- Butter, 50g (about 1.76 ounces)
- Garlic, minced, 10g (about 0.35 ounces)
- Lemon juice, 30ml (about 1 ounce)
- Fresh parsley, chopped, 20g (about 0.7 ounces)
- Salt and pepper to taste

Instructions:

Step 1: In a large skillet, melt butter over medium heat.

Step 2: Add garlic and sauté for 1 minute.

Step 3: Add shrimp and asparagus, cooking until the shrimp are pink and opaque.

Step 4: Stir in lemon juice and parsley, and season with salt and pepper.

Step 5: Cook for an additional 2-3 minutes, ensuring everything is heated through.

Step 6: Serve hot.

7. Keto Beef Stroganoff

Yields: 4 servings

Time: 30 minutes

Calories per serving: 550 Kcal

Ingredients:

- 600 gr or 21 oz beef sirloin, thinly sliced
- 200 gr or 7 oz white mushrooms, sliced
- 1 medium onion, finely chopped (approx. 100 gr or 3.5 oz)
- 240 ml or 8 oz beef broth
- 120 ml or 4 oz heavy cream
- 30 gr or 1 oz butter
- 1 tablespoon Dijon mustard
- Salt and pepper to taste
- Fresh parsley, chopped for garnish

Instructions:

Step 1: Melt butter in a large skillet over medium heat. Quickly brown the beef slices on both sides. Remove and set aside.

Step 2: In the same skillet, add onions and mushrooms, sautéing until they are soft and browned.

Step 3: Return the beef to the skillet and add beef broth. Bring to a simmer and reduce the liquid by half.

Step 4: Stir in heavy cream and Dijon mustard, simmering until the sauce thickens slightly. Season with salt and pepper.

Step 5: Serve garnished with fresh parsley. Ideal with a side of steamed green beans or keto-friendly noodles.

8. Keto Lemon Garlic Butter Shrimp with Asparagus

Yields: 4 servings

Time: 20 minutes

Calories per serving: 320 Kcal

Ingredients:

- 450 gr or 16 oz shrimp, peeled and deveined
- 300 gr or 10.5 oz asparagus, trimmed and cut into pieces
- 50 gr or 1.76 oz butter
- 1 lemon, zest, and juice (approx. 30 ml or 1 oz juice)
- 3 cloves garlic, minced (approx. 15 gr or 0.5 oz)
- Salt and pepper to taste
- Fresh parsley, chopped for garnish

Instructions:

Step 1: Melt butter in a large skillet over medium-high heat. Add garlic and lemon zest, and sauté for about 1 minute until fragrant.

Step 2: Add the shrimp and asparagus to the skillet. Cook for 5-7 minutes, stirring occasionally, until the shrimp are pink and opaque.

Step 3: Drizzle with lemon juice and season with salt and pepper.

Step 4: Serve hot, garnished with fresh parsley.

9. Keto Garlic Herb Roasted Duck

Yields: 4 servings

Time: Prep time: 20 minutes, Cook time: 1 hour 30 minutes

Calories per serving: 460 Kcal

Ingredients:

- 1 whole duck (approx. 2.2 kg or 5 lbs)
- 4 cloves garlic, minced
- 1 tablespoon fresh rosemary, finely chopped
- 1 tablespoon fresh thyme, finely chopped
- 2 tablespoons olive oil
- Salt and pepper, to taste
- 1 lemon, halved
- 100 ml (about 3.4 oz) dry white wine (optional, for added flavor)

Instructions:

Step 1: Preheat the Oven. Set your oven to 350°F (175°C).

Step 2: Prepare the Duck. Remove any giblets from the duck and pat dry with paper towels. Season the cavity with salt and pepper. Place the halved lemon inside the cavity.

Step 3: Make the Herb Mixture. In a small bowl, mix the minced garlic, rosemary, thyme, salt, and pepper with olive oil to create a paste.

Step 4: Season the Duck. Rub the outside of the duck with the herb mixture, ensuring it is evenly coated. You can gently lift the skin and rub some of the mixture directly on the meat for a deeper flavor.

Step 5: Roast the Duck. Place the duck breast side up on a rack in a roasting pan. If using white wine, pour it around the duck in the pan. Roast in the preheated oven for about 1 hour and 30 minutes.

10. Keto Smoked Salmon Frittata

Yields: 4 servings

Time: 25 minutes

Calories per serving: 300 Kcal

Ingredients:

- 200 gr or 7 oz smoked salmon, roughly chopped
- 6 large eggs
- 100 gr or 3.5 oz cream cheese, cubed
- 50 gr or 1.76 oz fresh dill, chopped
- Salt and pepper to taste
- Butter for greasing

Instructions:

Step 1: Preheat your oven to 350°F (175°C). Grease a pie dish with butter.

Step 2: In a bowl, whisk the eggs and season with salt and pepper.

Step 3: Pour the eggs into the prepared dish. Add chunks of cream cheese and smoked salmon evenly throughout the egg mixture.

Step 4: Bake for 18-20 minutes until the eggs are set and the top is slightly golden.

Step 5: Garnish with fresh dill before serving.

11. Keto Garlic Butter Pork Tenderloin

Yields: 4 servings

Time: 45 minutes

Calories per serving: 505 Kcal

Ingredients:

- 1 pork tenderloin (approx. 800 gr or 28 oz)
- 50 gr or 1.76 oz butter
- 4 cloves garlic, minced (approx. 20 gr or 0.7 oz)
- 1 tablespoon fresh rosemary, chopped
- Salt and pepper to taste

Instructions:

Step 1: Preheat the oven to 375°F (190°C).

Step 2: Season the pork tenderloin with salt and pepper.

Step 3: In a skillet, melt the butter over medium heat. Add garlic and rosemary, sautéing for 1-2 minutes until fragrant.

Step 4: Sear the pork tenderloin in the skillet, browning on all sides.

Step 5: Transfer the skillet to the oven and roast for 20-25 minutes until a meat thermometer reads 145°F (63°C).

Step 6: Let the pork rest for 5 minutes before slicing. Serve with a spoonful of the garlic butter from the skillet.

12. Keto Mediterranean Chicken Skillet

Yields: 4 servings

Time: 30 minutes

Calories per serving: 460 Kcal

Ingredients:
- 4 chicken breasts (approx. 800 gr or 28 oz total)
- 100 gr or 3.5 oz of feta cheese, crumbled
- 150 gr or 5.3 oz cherry tomatoes, halved
- 100 gr or 3.5 oz black olives, pitted and halved
- 60 ml or 2 oz extra virgin olive oil
- 30 gr or 1 oz fresh basil leaves
- 2 cloves garlic, minced (approx. 10 gr or 0.35 oz)
- Salt and pepper to taste

Instructions:

Step 1: Heat olive oil in a large skillet over medium heat. Season chicken breasts with salt and pepper, and sear until golden, about 5 minutes on each side.

Step 2: Reduce the heat and add garlic, cherry tomatoes, and olives to the skillet. Cook for 5-7 minutes until the tomatoes are slightly softened.

Step 3: Sprinkle feta cheese and basil over the chicken. Cover and cook for another 5-10 minutes until chicken is cooked through.

Step 4: Serve hot, garnished with additional basil if desired.

13. Keto Herb-Crusted Pork Chops

Yields: 4 servings

Time: 25 minutes

Calories per serving: 530 Kcal

Ingredients:

- 4 pork chops (approx. 800 gr or 28 oz total)
- 50 gr or 1.76 oz Parmesan cheese, grated
- 50 gr or 1.76 oz almond flour
- 20 gr or 0.7 oz fresh rosemary, finely chopped
- 20 gr or 0.7 oz fresh thyme, finely chopped
- 2 cloves garlic, minced (approx. 10 gr or 0.35 oz)
- 60 ml or 2 oz olive oil

Instructions:

Step 1: Preheat your oven to 400°F (200°C).

Step 2: In a bowl, mix Parmesan cheese, almond flour, rosemary, thyme, and garlic.

Step 3: Season pork chops with salt and pepper. Brush each chop with olive oil, then press the herb mixture onto each side.

Step 4: Heat a skillet over medium-high heat, add pork chops, and sear each side for 2-3 minutes.

Step 5: Transfer pork chops to a baking tray and bake in the oven for 10-15 minutes until cooked through.

Step 6: Serve hot, with a side of sautéed green beans.

14. Keto Cauliflower and Cheese Bake

Yields: 4 servings

Time: 40 minutes

Calories per serving: 370 Kcal

Ingredients:

- 600 gr or 21 oz cauliflower florets
- 200 gr or 7 oz cream cheese
- 100 gr or 3.5 oz cheddar cheese, shredded
- 100 ml or 3.4 oz heavy cream
- 50 gr or 1.76 oz Parmesan cheese, grated
- 2 cloves garlic, minced (approx. 10 gr or 0.35 oz)
- Salt and pepper to taste
- Butter for greasing

Instructions:

Step 1: Preheat your oven to 350°F (175°C). Grease a baking dish with butter.

Step 2: Steam cauliflower florets until tender, about 7-8 minutes. Drain and set aside.

Step 3: In a saucepan, mix cream cheese, cheddar cheese, heavy cream, and garlic. Heat until the cheeses melt and the mixture is smooth.

Step 4: Add steamed cauliflower to the cheese mixture, stirring gently to coat. Season with salt and pepper.

Step 5: Transfer the cauliflower and cheese mixture to the prepared baking dish. Sprinkle with Parmesan cheese.

Step 6: Bake for 20-25 minutes, until bubbly and golden on top.

Step 7: Serve hot, garnished with fresh herbs if desired.

15. Keto Spicy Shrimp and Avocado Salad

Yields: 4 servings

Time: 20 minutes

Calories per serving: 400 Kcal

Ingredients:

- 450 gr or 16 oz shrimp, peeled and deveined
- 2 ripe avocados, diced (approx. 300 gr or 10.5 oz total)
- 100 gr or 3.5 oz cherry tomatoes, halved
- 50 gr or 1.76 oz red onion, finely chopped
- 1 jalapeño, seeded and finely chopped (approx. 15 gr or 0.5 oz)
- Juice of 1 lime (approx. 30 ml or 1 oz)
- 30 ml or 1 oz olive oil
- Salt and pepper to taste and fresh cilantro, chopped for garnish

Instructions:

Step 1: In a large bowl, combine shrimp, avocado, cherry tomatoes, red onion, and jalapeño.

Step 2: In a small bowl, whisk together lime juice, olive oil, salt, and pepper.

Step 3: Pour dressing over the shrimp mixture and gently toss to combine.

Step 4: Refrigerate for 10 minutes to allow flavors to meld.

Step 5: Serve chilled, garnished with fresh cilantro.

16. Keto Garlic and Herb Grilled Lamb Chops

Yields: 4 servings

Time: 25 minutes

Calories per serving: 480 Kcal

Ingredients:

- 8 lamb chops (approx. 800 gr or 28 oz total)
- 30 gr or 1 oz fresh rosemary, finely chopped
- 30 gr or 1 oz fresh thyme, finely chopped
- 4 cloves garlic, minced (approx. 20 gr or 0.7 oz)
- 60 ml or 2 oz olive oil
- Salt and pepper to taste

Instructions:

Step 1: In a small bowl, mix rosemary, thyme, garlic, and olive oil to create a marinade.

Step 2: Season the lamb chops with salt and pepper, then coat them with the herb marinade. Let them sit for at least 15 minutes.

Step 3: Preheat the grill to medium-high heat. Grill lamb chops for 3-4 minutes per side or until they reach desired doneness.

Step 4: Rest lamb chops for 5 minutes before serving.

17. Keto Duck Breast with Red Wine Reduction

Yields: 4 servings

Time: 45 minutes

Calories per serving: 510 Kcal

Ingredients:

- 4 duck breasts (approx. 800 gr or 28 oz total)
- Salt and pepper to taste
- 200 ml or 6.8 oz red wine (choose a low-carb option)
- 2 cloves garlic, minced (approx. 10 gr or 0.35 oz)
- 30 ml or 1 oz balsamic vinegar
- 10 gr or 0.35 oz fresh thyme

Instructions:

Step 1: Preheat the oven to 400°F (200°C). Score the duck skin in a crisscross pattern and season with salt and pepper.

Step 2: Place duck breasts skin side down in a cold non-stick skillet. Turn heat to medium and cook until the fat is rendered and the skin is golden and crispy, for about 6-8 minutes.

Step 3: Flip the duck breasts and cook for an additional 2 minutes. Then, transfer to the oven and roast for 6-8 minutes for medium-rare.

Step 4: Remove the duck from the oven, cover with foil, and let it rest. Pour off most of the fat from the skillet, add garlic, red wine, balsamic vinegar, and thyme, and bring to a simmer until reduced by half.

Step 5: Slice duck breasts and serve with the red wine reduction.

18. Keto Coconut Curry Chicken

Yields: 4 servings

Time: 35 minutes

Calories per serving: 495 Kcal

Ingredients:

- 800 gr or 28 oz chicken thighs, boneless and skinless, cut into pieces
- 200 ml or 6.8 oz coconut milk
- 100 gr or 3.5 oz red bell pepper, sliced
- 100 gr or 3.5 oz onion, chopped
- 50 gr or 1.76 oz tomato paste
- 30 gr or 1 oz fresh ginger, minced
- 2 cloves garlic, minced (approx. 10 gr or 0.35 oz)
- 15 ml or 0.5 oz olive oil
- 15 gr or 0.5 oz curry powder
- Salt and pepper to taste
- Fresh cilantro, chopped for garnish

Instructions:

Step 1: Heat olive oil in a large skillet over medium heat. Sauté onion, bell pepper, ginger, and garlic until translucent.

Step 2: Add chicken pieces to the skillet and season with salt, pepper, and curry powder. Cook until chicken is browned.

Step 3: Stir in tomato paste and coconut milk, and simmer. Reduce heat and let simmer for 20 minutes, until the chicken is tender and the sauce has thickened.

Step 4: Serve hot, garnished with fresh cilantro. For a complete keto meal, serve with a side of cauliflower rice. If you like you can make skewers with the chicken

19. Keto Walnut-Crusted Pork Tenderloin

Yields: 4 servings

Time: 45 minutes

Calories per serving: 520 Kcal

Ingredients:

- 800 gr or 28 oz pork tenderloin
- 100 gr or 3.5 oz walnuts, finely chopped
- 1 egg, beaten
- 30 ml or 1 oz Dijon mustard
- Salt and pepper to taste
- Olive oil for cooking

Instructions:

Step 1: Preheat your oven to 375°F (190°C).

Step 2: Season the pork tenderloin with salt and pepper, then brush it all over with Dijon mustard.

Step 3: Dip the mustard-coated tenderloin in a beaten egg, then roll it in chopped walnuts until fully coated.

Step 4: Heat olive oil in an oven-proof skillet over medium-high heat. Sear the pork tenderloin on all sides until golden.

Step 5: Transfer the skillet to the oven and roast for 25-30 minutes, or until the pork reaches an internal temperature of 145°F (63°C).

Step 6: Let rest for 5 minutes before slicing. Serve warm.

20. Keto Lemon Herb Roasted Chicken

Yields: 4 servings

Time: 1 hour 20 minutes

Calories per serving: 460 Kcal

Ingredients:

- 1 whole chicken (approx. 1200 gr or 42 oz)
- 1 lemon, halved
- 30 gr or 1 oz fresh rosemary
- 30 gr or 1 oz fresh thyme
- 60 ml or 2 oz olive oil
- Salt and pepper to taste

Instructions:

Step 1: Preheat your oven to 425°F (220°C).

Step 2: Rub the chicken with olive oil, salt, and pepper. Stuff the cavity with lemon halves, rosemary, and thyme.

Step 3: Place the chicken in a roasting pan and roast for 1 hour and 10 minutes, or until the juices run clear when you cut between a leg and thigh.

Step 4: Remove from the oven, cover with aluminum foil, and rest for 10 minutes before carving.

Step 5: Serve the chicken with a side of roasted keto vegetables like Brussels sprouts or zucchini.

21. Keto Spicy Beef Stir-Fry

Yields: 4 servings

Time: 30 minutes

Calories per serving: 400 Kcal

Ingredients:

- 600 gr or 21 oz beef strips
- 200 gr or 7 oz broccoli florets
- 100 gr or 3.5 oz red bell pepper, sliced
- 50 gr or 1.76 oz green onions, sliced
- 30 ml or 1 oz soy sauce (ensure it's gluten-free for keto)
- 30 ml or 1 oz sesame oil
- 5 gr or 0.18 oz crushed red pepper flakes (adjust to taste)
- Salt and pepper to taste

Instructions:

Step 1: Heat sesame oil in a large skillet over high heat. Add beef strips and stir-fry until they brown, about 3-5 minutes.

Step 2: Add broccoli and bell pepper to the skillet and stir-fry for another 5-7 minutes until vegetables are tender-crisp.

Step 3: Stir in soy sauce, green onions, and red pepper flakes. Cook for another 2 minutes until everything is heated through and coated in sauce.

Step 4: Season with salt and pepper to taste. Serve hot.

22. Keto Smoked Salmon and Avocado Towers

Yields: 4 servings
Time: 20 minutes
Calories per serving: 300 Kcal

Ingredients:

- 300 gr or 10.5 oz smoked salmon, sliced
- 2 avocados, peeled and mashed (approx. 300 gr or 10.5 oz total)
- 50 gr or 1.76 oz cream cheese
- 15 ml or 0.5 oz lemon juice
- Fresh dill, chopped for garnish
- Salt and pepper to taste

Instructions:

Step 1: In a bowl, mix mashed avocado, cream cheese, lemon juice, salt, and pepper until smooth.

Step 2: Layer the avocado mixture and smoked salmon using a small ring mold or a cup, pressing lightly to form a tower.

Step 3: Carefully remove the mold. Repeat for the remaining servings.

Step 4: Garnish with chopped dill. Serve immediately.

23. Keto Parmesan-Crusted Halibut

Yields: 4 servings

Time: 25 minutes

Calories per serving: 420 Kcal

Ingredients:

- 4 halibut fillets (approx. 800 gr or 28 oz total)
- 100 gr or 3.5 oz grated Parmesan cheese
- 50 gr or 1.76 oz almond flour
- 1 egg, beaten
- 30 ml or 1 oz olive oil
- Salt and pepper to taste
- Lemon wedges for serving

Instructions:

Step 1: Preheat your oven to 400°F (200°C).

Step 2: Mix Parmesan cheese and almond flour in a shallow dish.

Step 3: Dip each halibut fillet in a beaten egg, then coat it with the Parmesan mixture.

Step 4: Heat olive oil in an oven-safe skillet over medium heat. Sear the fillets for 2 minutes on each side until golden.

Step 5: Transfer the skillet to the oven and bake for 10 minutes or until the fish flakes easily.

Step 6: Serve hot with lemon wedges on the side.

24. Keto Ratatouille with Grilled Chicken

Yields: 4 servings

Time: 45 minutes

Calories per serving: 380 Kcal

Ingredients:

- 4 chicken breasts (approx. 800 gr or 28 oz total)
- 100 gr or 3.5 oz eggplant, sliced
- 100 gr or 3.5 oz zucchini, sliced
- 100 gr or 3.5 oz bell peppers, mixed colors, sliced
- 100 gr or 3.5 oz tomatoes, diced
- 30 ml or 1 oz olive oil
- 2 cloves garlic, minced (approx. 10 gr or 0.35 oz)
- 10 gr or 0.35 oz fresh basil, chopped
- Salt and pepper to taste

Instructions:

Step 1: Season chicken breasts with salt and pepper, grill over medium heat until fully cooked, about 6-7 minutes per side.

Step 2: Heat olive oil over medium heat in a large pan. Sauté garlic for 1 minute.

Step 3: Add all vegetables to the pan and cook until tender, about 15 minutes. Stir in basil and season with salt and pepper.

Step 4: Serve grilled chicken on a bed of ratatouille.

25. Keto Stuffed Avocados with Crabmeat

Yields: 4 servings

Time: 20 minutes

Calories per serving: 320 Kcal

Ingredients:

- 4 avocados, halved and pitted (approx. 800 gr or 28 oz total)
- 200 gr or 7 oz crabmeat, cooked
- 50 gr or 1.76 oz mayonnaise
- 20 gr or 0.7 oz celery, finely chopped
- 15 ml or 0.5 oz lemon juice
- Salt and pepper to taste
- Fresh dill for garnish

Instructions:

Step 1: Scoop out some of the avocado flesh, leaving a shell.

Step 2: In a bowl, mix crabmeat, mayonnaise, celery, lemon juice, and the scooped avocado. Season with salt and pepper.

Step 3: Spoon the mixture back into the avocado shells.

Step 4: Garnish with fresh dill and serve.

26. Keto Mushroom and Swiss Chard Stuffed Pork Tenderloin

Yields: 4 servings

Time: 1 hour

Calories per serving: 530 Kcal

Ingredients:

- 1 pork tenderloin (approx. 800 gr or 28 oz)
- 100 gr or 3.5 oz mushrooms, finely chopped
- 100 gr or 3.5 oz Swiss chard, chopped
- 50 gr or 1.76 oz onions, chopped
- 2 cloves garlic, minced (approx. 10 gr or 0.35 oz)
- 30 ml or 1 oz olive oil
- Salt and pepper to taste

Instructions:

Step 1: Preheat your oven to 375°F (190°C).

Step 2: Butterfly the pork tenderloin to flatten.

Step 3: Heat olive oil over medium heat in a pan. Sauté onions, mushrooms, garlic, and Swiss chard until soft. Season with salt and pepper.

Step 4: Spread the vegetable mixture over the tenderloin, roll it up, and secure with kitchen twine.

Step 5: Roast in the oven for 35-40 minutes or until the pork reaches an internal temperature of 145°F (63°C).

Step 6: Let rest for 10 minutes, remove twine, slice, and serve.

27. Keto Thai Coconut Shrimp Soup

Yields: 4 servings

Time: 30 minutes

Calories per serving: 350 Kcal

Ingredients:

- 450 gr or 16 oz shrimp, peeled and deveined
- 400 ml or 13.5 oz coconut milk
- 200 ml or 6.8 oz chicken broth
- 100 gr or 3.5 oz mushrooms, sliced
- 50 gr or 1.76 oz red bell pepper, sliced
- 1 stalk lemongrass, minced (approx. 10 gr or 0.35 oz)
- 30 ml or 1 oz fish sauce
- 5 gr or 0.18 oz fresh ginger, minced
- Fresh cilantro for garnish
- Salt and pepper to taste

Instructions:

Step 1: In a large pot, bring coconut milk, chicken broth, lemongrass, and ginger to a simmer.

Step 2: Add bell peppers and mushrooms and cook for 5 minutes.

Step 3: Add shrimp and cook until they are pink and opaque about 3-5 minutes. Stir in fish sauce.

Step 4: Season with salt and pepper, garnish with fresh cilantro, and serve hot.

28. Keto Lemon Butter Seared Scallops

Yields: 4 servings

Time: 20 minutes

Calories per serving: 310 Kcal

Ingredients:

- 400 gr or 14 oz scallops
- 30 gr or 1 oz butter
- Juice of 1 lemon (approx. 30 ml or 1 oz)
- Salt and pepper to taste
- Fresh parsley, chopped for garnish

Instructions:

Step 1: Pat scallops dry and season with salt and pepper.

Step 2: Heat butter in a skillet over high heat until foaming. Sear scallops on each side for about 1-2 minutes until golden and translucent.

Step 3: Remove from heat, squeeze lemon juice over scallops, and garnish with parsley.

Step 4: Serve immediately.

29. Keto Cauliflower Steak with Chimichurri Sauce

Yields: 4 servings

Time: 30 minutes

Calories per serving: 250 Kcal

Ingredients:

- 2 large heads of cauliflower (approx. 800 gr or 28 oz total), sliced into 'steaks'
- 30 ml or 1 oz olive oil
- Salt and pepper to taste
- **For the Chimichurri:**
  - 50 gr or 1.76 oz fresh parsley, chopped
  - 10 gr or 0.35 oz fresh oregano, chopped
  - 1 clove garlic, minced (approx. 5 gr or 0.18 oz)
  - 60 ml or 2 oz olive oil
  - 15 ml or 0.5 oz red wine vinegar
  - Red pepper flakes, a pinch

Instructions:

Step 1: Preheat your oven to 400°F (200°C).

Step 2: Brush cauliflower steaks with olive oil, season with salt and pepper, and roast in the oven for about 20-25 minutes until tender and golden.

Step 3: For the chimichurri, mix all ingredients in a bowl.

Step 4: Serve cauliflower steaks drizzled with chimichurri sauce.

30. Keto Bacon-Wrapped Asparagus with Hollandaise

Yields: 4 servings

Time: 35 minutes

Calories per serving: 390 Kcal

Ingredients:
- 16 asparagus spears (approx. 400 gr or 14 oz)
- 8 slices of bacon (approx. 225 gr or 8 oz)
- **For the Hollandaise:**
    - 2 egg yolks
    - 120 gr or 4 oz butter, melted
    - 15 ml or 0.5 oz lemon juice
    - Salt and cayenne pepper to taste

Instructions:

Step 1: Preheat your oven to 400°F (200°C).

Step 2: Wrap each asparagus spear with half a slice of bacon and place on a baking sheet.

Step 3: Roast for 20-25 minutes until the bacon is crispy.

Step 4: For the hollandaise, whisk egg yolks, lemon juice, and a splash of water over low heat until pale and thick. Slowly whisk in melted butter until the sauce is creamy. Season with salt and cayenne pepper.

Step 5: Serve asparagus wrapped in bacon with hollandaise sauce drizzled over the top.

Chapter 9: Treats and Snacks: Keto Desserts and Snacks

1. Keto Chocolate Mousse

Yields: 4 servings

Time: 15 minutes

Calories per serving: 310 Kcal

Ingredients:

- 200 ml or 6.8 oz heavy cream
- 100 gr or 3.5 oz unsweetened dark chocolate, melted
- 30 gr or 1 oz erythritol (or suitable keto sweetener)
- 1 tsp vanilla extract
- A pinch of salt

Instructions:

Step 1: In a mixing bowl, whip the heavy cream with erythritol, vanilla extract, and a pinch of salt until stiff peaks form.

Step 2: Gently fold in the melted chocolate until well combined.

Step 3: Spoon the mousse into serving dishes and refrigerate for at least an hour before serving.

2. Keto Lemon Bars

Yields: 8 servings

Time: 50 minutes

Calories per serving: 200 Kcal

Ingredients:
- For the crust:
  - 150 gr or 5.3 oz almond flour
  - 50 gr or 1.76 oz butter, melted
  - 15 gr or 0.5 oz erythritol
- For the filling:
  - 3 eggs
  - 120 ml or 4 oz fresh lemon juice
  - 100 gr or 3.5 oz erythritol
  - Zest of 1 lemon

Instructions:

Step 1: Preheat the oven to 350°F (175°C). Mix the almond flour, melted butter, and erythritol to form the crust. Press it into the bottom of a lined baking pan. Bake for 15 minutes.

Step 2: Whisk together eggs, lemon juice, erythritol, and lemon zest. Pour over the pre-baked crust.

Step 3: Return to the oven and bake for 20-25 minutes until the filling is set.

Step 4: Cool completely before cutting into bars. Refrigerate until ready to serve.

3. Keto Cheesecake Bites

Yields: 12 servings
Time: 1 hour (plus chilling)
Calories per serving: 220 Kcal

Ingredients:

- 200 gr or 7 oz cream cheese, softened
- 100 gr or 3.5 oz sour cream
- 50 gr or 1.76 oz erythritol
- 1 egg
- 1 tsp vanilla extract
- Almond flour for dusting

Instructions:

Step 1: Preheat oven to 300°F (150°C). Line a mini muffin tin with paper liners.

Step 2: Beat together cream cheese, sour cream, erythritol, egg, and vanilla extract until smooth.

Step 3: Pour mixture into prepared muffin tin, filling each about three-quarters full.

Step 4: Bake for 20-25 minutes or until set. Cool and then refrigerate for at least 2 hours.

Step 5: Dust with almond flour before serving.

4. Keto Coconut Clusters

Yields: 6 servings

Time: 20 minutes

Calories per serving: 180 Kcal

Ingredients:

- 100 gr or 3.5 oz unsweetened shredded coconut
- 50 gr or 1.76 oz sliced almonds
- 30 ml or 1 oz coconut oil
- 30 gr or 1 oz erythritol
- A pinch of salt

Instructions:

Step 1: Preheat oven to 325°F (165°C). Mix all ingredients in a bowl until well coated.

Step 2: Spoon small clusters onto a baking sheet lined with parchment paper.

Step 3: Bake for 10-12 minutes or until golden. Let cool completely before serving.

5. Keto Peanut Butter Cups

Yields: 8 servings

Time: 30 minutes (plus chilling)

Calories per serving: 210 Kcal

Ingredients:

- 100 gr or 3.5 oz sugar-free dark chocolate, melted
- 100 gr or 3.5 oz natural peanut butter, smooth
- 20 gr or 0.7 oz erythritol

Instructions:

Step 1: Line a mini muffin tin with paper liners. Spoon a layer of melted chocolate into each liner. Freeze for 5 minutes.

Step 2: Mix peanut butter with erythritol. Spoon a small amount onto the hardened chocolate. Freeze for another 5 minutes.

Step 3: Cover with remaining chocolate and freeze until set.

Step 4: Keep refrigerated until ready to serve.

6. Keto Almond Joy Bars

Yields: 8 servings

Time: 35 minutes (plus chilling)

Calories per serving: 230 Kcal

Ingredients:

- 100 gr or 3.5 oz unsweetened shredded coconut
- 30 ml or 1 oz coconut cream
- 30 gr or 1 oz erythritol
- 100 gr or 3.5 oz sugar-free dark chocolate, melted
- 30 gr or 1 oz almonds

Instructions:

Step 1: Mix shredded coconut with coconut cream and erythritol. Form into small bars and press an almond into each. Freeze for 15 minutes.

Step 2: Dip each bar into melted chocolate, ensuring full coverage. Freeze until the chocolate sets.

Step 3: Store in the refrigerator until ready to serve.

7. Keto Cinnamon Roll Fat Bombs

Yields: 10 servings

Time: 20 minutes (plus chilling)

Calories per serving: 150 Kcal

Ingredients:

- 100 gr or 3.5 oz cream cheese, softened
- 50 gr or 1.76 oz butter, softened
- 30 gr or 1 oz erythritol
- 5 gr or 0.18 oz ground cinnamon

Instructions:

Step 1: Beat cream cheese, butter, erythritol, and cinnamon until smooth.

Step 2: Chill the mixture until firm enough to handle, then form into small balls.

Step 3: Refrigerate until firm, about 1 hour. Serve chilled.

8. Keto Raspberry Gelatin Dessert

Yields: 4 servings
Time: 10 minutes (plus setting time)
Calories per serving: 50 Kcal

Ingredients:

- 400 ml or 13.5 oz water
- 10 gr or 0.35 oz unflavored gelatin powder
- 100 gr or 3.5 oz fresh raspberries
- 20 gr or 0.7 oz erythritol

Instructions:

Step 1: Heat half the water to a boil and dissolve the gelatin and erythritol.

Step 2: Add the remaining water and raspberries, gently mashing the berries.

Step 3: Pour into molds or a dish and refrigerate until set about 3-4 hours.

Step 4: Serve chilled.

9. Keto Chocolate Avocado Truffles

Yields: 8 servings

Time: 15 minutes (plus chilling)

Calories per serving: 200 Kcal

Ingredients:

- 2 ripe avocados (approx. 400 gr or 14 oz total)
- 100 gr or 3.5 oz unsweetened dark chocolate, melted
- 30 gr or 1 oz cocoa powder for dusting
- 30 gr or 1 oz erythritol, powdered
- 1 tsp vanilla extract

Instructions:

Step 1: Puree the avocados in a food processor until smooth.

Step 2: Add melted chocolate, erythritol, and vanilla extract, blending until well combined.

Step 3: Chill the mixture in the refrigerator for at least 1 hour until it firms up.

Step 4: Form the mixture into small balls, then roll each in cocoa powder to coat.

Step 5: Chill the truffles again before serving.

10. Keto Mini Blueberry Cheesecakes

Yields: 12 servings

Time: 30 minutes (plus chilling)

Calories per serving: 180 Kcal

Ingredients:

- 200 gr or 7 oz cream cheese, softened
- 50 gr or 1.76 oz sour cream
- 50 gr or 1.76 oz erythritol
- 1 egg
- 1 tsp vanilla extract
- 100 gr or 3.5 oz fresh blueberries

Instructions:

Step 1: Preheat oven to 350°F (175°C). Line a mini muffin tin with paper liners.

Step 2: Beat cream cheese, sour cream, erythritol, egg, and vanilla extract in a bowl until smooth.

Step 3: Divide the mixture among the muffin cups. Press a few blueberries into each.

Step 4: Bake for 15-20 minutes or until set. Chill in the refrigerator for at least 2 hours before serving.

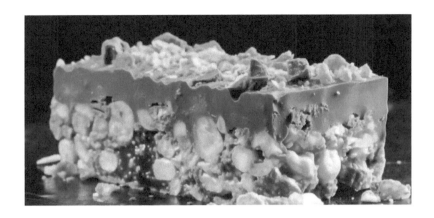

11. Keto Salted Caramel Pecan Bark

Yields: 8 servings

Time: 20 minutes (plus cooling)

Calories per serving: 220 Kcal

Ingredients:

- 150 gr or 5.3 oz sugar-free dark chocolate, melted
- 50 gr or 1.76 oz pecans, chopped
- 50 ml or 1.7 oz sugar-free caramel sauce
- Sea salt for sprinkling

Instructions:

Step 1: Line a baking sheet with parchment paper.

Step 2: Spread the melted chocolate into a thin layer on the parchment paper.

Step 3: Drizzle caramel sauce over the chocolate and sprinkle with chopped pecans and a little sea salt.

Step 4: Chill in the refrigerator until set, about 1 hour. Break into pieces before serving.

12. Keto Coconut Lime Fat Bombs

Yields: 10 servings

Time: 15 minutes (plus freezing)

Calories per serving: 150 Kcal

Ingredients:

- 200 gr or 7 oz coconut butter
- 30 ml or 1 oz coconut oil
- Zest and juice of 1 lime (approx. 15 ml or 0.5 oz juice)
- 30 gr or 1 oz erythritol, powdered
- Unsweetened shredded coconut for coating

Instructions:

Step 1: Melt coconut butter and coconut oil together in a saucepan over low heat.

Step 2: Remove from heat and stir in lime zest, lime juice, and erythritol until well combined.

Step 3: Pour the mixture into molds or drop by spoonfuls onto a parchment-lined tray.

Step 4: Freeze until set, about 1 hour. Roll in shredded coconut before serving.

13. Keto Parmesan Crisps

Yields: 4 servings

Time: 15 minutes

Calories per serving: 100 Kcal

Ingredients:

- 100 gr or 3.5 oz grated Parmesan cheese

Instructions:

Step 1: Preheat your oven to 400°F (200°C).

Step 2: Line a baking sheet with parchment paper. Spoon tablespoons of Parmesan onto the baking sheet, spreading them out into thin circles.

Step 3: Bake for 5-7 minutes or until golden and crisp.

Step 4: Allow to cool on the baking sheet before serving.

14. Keto Rosemary Garlic Flaxseed Crackers

Yields: 6 servings

Time: 30 minutes

Calories per serving: 150 Kcal

Ingredients:

- 100 gr or 3.5 oz flaxseed meal
- 30 ml or 1 oz water
- 10 gr or 0.35 oz fresh rosemary, finely chopped
- 2 cloves garlic, minced (approx. 10 gr or 0.35 oz)
- Salt to taste

Instructions:

Step 1: Preheat oven to 350°F (175°C).

Step 2: Mix all ingredients in a bowl until a dough forms.

Step 3: Roll out the dough between two sheets of parchment paper to 1/8-inch thickness. Remove the top sheet and cut the dough into squares with a knife.

Step 4: Bake for 20-25 minutes or until crisp and golden. Break along cut lines.

Step 5: Let cool completely before serving.

15. Keto Spicy Pumpkin Seeds

Yields: 4 servings

Time: 25 minutes

Calories per serving: 180 Kcal

Ingredients:

- 200 gr or 7 oz pumpkin seeds
- 15 ml or 0.5 oz olive oil
- 5 gr or 0.18 oz chili powder
- Salt to taste

Instructions:

Step 1: Preheat your oven to 300°F (150°C).

Step 2: Toss the pumpkin seeds with olive oil, chili powder, and salt in a bowl.

Step 3: Spread the seeds in a single layer on a baking sheet.

Step 4: Bake for about 20 minutes, stirring occasionally, until toasted and crispy.

Step 5: Let cool before serving.

16. Keto Avocado Chips

Yields: 4 servings

Time: 30 minutes

Calories per serving: 140 Kcal

Ingredients:

- 1 large ripe avocado (approx. 200 gr or 7 oz)
- 50 gr or 1.76 oz grated Parmesan cheese
- 1 tsp lemon juice
- Garlic powder and chili flakes to taste

Instructions:

Step 1: Preheat your oven to 350°F (175°C). Line a baking sheet with parchment paper.

Step 2: Mash the avocado with lemon juice, Parmesan, garlic powder, and chili flakes.

Step 3: Spoon dollops of the mixture onto the baking sheet, flattening into thin circles.

Step 4: Bake for 15-20 minutes or until crisp and golden.

Step 5: Cool on the baking sheet before serving.

17. Keto Cheese and Herb Stuffed Mushrooms

Yields: 4 servings

Time: 30 minutes

Calories per serving: 160 Kcal

Ingredients:

- 12 whole large mushrooms (approx. 300 gr or 10.5 oz)
- 100 gr or 3.5 oz cream cheese, softened
- 50 gr or 1.76 oz shredded cheddar cheese
- 10 gr or 0.35 oz fresh herbs (parsley, thyme), chopped
- Salt and pepper to taste

Instructions:

Step 1: Preheat the oven to 375°F (190°C). Remove the stems from the mushrooms and finely chop them.

Step 2: Mix chopped stems with cream cheese, cheddar, herbs, salt, and pepper.

Step 3: Stuff mushroom caps with the mixture and place on a baking sheet.

Step 4: Bake for 20 minutes or until the mushrooms are tender and the filling is golden.

Step 5: Serve warm.

18. Keto Bacon-Wrapped Jalapeño Poppers

Yields: 4 servings

Time: 40 minutes

Calories per serving: 200 Kcal

Ingredients:

- 8 jalapeño peppers (approx. 200 gr or 7 oz)
- 100 gr or 3.5 oz cream cheese, softened
- 8 slices bacon (approx. 225 gr or 8 oz)

Instructions:

Step 1: Preheat oven to 400°F (200°C). Cut jalapeños in half lengthwise and remove seeds.

Step 2: Fill each jalapeño half with cream cheese.

Step 3: Wrap each stuffed jalapeño with a slice of bacon. Secure with a toothpick if necessary.

Step 4: Place on a baking sheet and bake for 20-25 minutes or until crispy.

Step 5: Serve warm.

19. Keto Olive Tapenade with Flaxseed Crackers

Yields: 6 servings

Time: 15 minutes

Calories per serving: 130 Kcal

Ingredients:

- 150 gr or 5.3 oz mixed olives, pitted and chopped
- 30 gr or 1 oz capers, rinsed and chopped
- 2 cloves garlic, minced (approx. 10 gr or 0.35 oz)
- 30 ml or 1 oz olive oil
- 5 gr or 0.18 oz fresh lemon juice
- 100 gr or 3.5 oz flaxseed crackers (homemade or store-bought)

Instructions:

Step 1: Mix olives, capers, garlic, olive oil, and lemon juice in a bowl until combined.

Step 2: Serve the tapenade with flaxseed crackers for dipping.

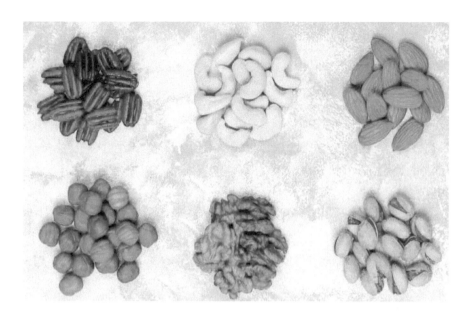

20. Keto Spiced Nuts

Yields: 4 servings

Time: 20 minutes

Calories per serving: 220 Kcal

Ingredients:

- 200 gr or 7 oz mixed nuts (almonds, walnuts, pecans)
- 15 ml or 0.5 oz olive oil
- 5 gr or 0.18 oz smoked paprika
- Salt and cayenne pepper to taste

Instructions:

Step 1: Preheat your oven to 350°F (175°C).

Step 2: In a bowl, toss the nuts with olive oil, smoked paprika, salt, and cayenne pepper.

Step 3: Spread the nuts on a baking sheet in a single layer.

Step 4: Bake for 10-15 minutes, stirring occasionally, until toasted and fragrant.

Step 5: Cool before serving.

Chapter 10: Celebratory Foods: Keto for Special Occasions

1. Keto Lobster Tail with Herb Butter

Yields: 4 servings

Time: 20 minutes

Calories per serving: 290 Kcal

Ingredients:
- 4 lobster tails (approx. 800 gr or 28 oz total)
- 100 gr or 3.5 oz butter, softened
- 10 gr or 0.35 oz fresh parsley, chopped
- 1 clove garlic, minced (approx. 5 gr or 0.18 oz)
- Zest of 1 lemon
- Salt and pepper to taste

Instructions:

Step 1: Preheat your broiler.

Step 2: Lose the lobster tails to expose the meat and place it on a baking sheet.

Step 3: In a small bowl, mix the butter, parsley, garlic, lemon zest, salt, and pepper.

Step 4: Spoon the butter mixture over the lobster meat.

Step 5: Broil for about 8-10 minutes or until the lobster is fully cooked and the butter is bubbling.

Step 6: Serve immediately, garnished with lemon wedges.

2. Keto Beef Wellington

Yields: 6 servings

Time: 1 hour 30 minutes

Calories per serving: 550 Kcal

Ingredients:

- 1 kg or 35 oz beef tenderloin
- 200 gr or 7 oz mushroom, finely chopped
- 50 gr or 1.76 oz onions, finely chopped
- 2 cloves garlic, minced (approx. 10 gr or 0.35 oz)
- 30 gr or 1 oz Dijon mustard
- 100 gr or 3.5 oz prosciutto slices
- 1 keto pastry dough (made with almond flour and xanthan gum)
- 1 egg, beaten for egg wash
- Salt and pepper to taste
- Olive oil

Instructions:

Step 1: Preheat oven to 400°F (200°C).

Step 2: Season the beef with salt and pepper. Sear all sides in a hot skillet with olive oil. Remove and let cool. Once cool, brush all over with mustard.

Step 3: In the same skillet, sauté onions, mushrooms, and garlic until all the moisture evaporates. Let cool.

Step 4: Lay out overlapping prosciutto slices on cling film. Spread the mushroom mixture over the prosciutto, then roll the beef in the mushrooms and prosciutto.

Step 5: Wrap the beef with the keto pastry dough, seal the edges, and brush with egg wash.

Step 6: Bake for about 30-40 minutes or until the pastry is golden. Let rest before slicing. Serve warm.

3. Keto Stuffed Capon

Yields: 8 servings

Time: 2 hours 30 minutes

Calories per serving: 400 Kcal

Ingredients:

- 1 whole capon (approx. 2.5 kg or 88 oz)
- 200 gr or 7 oz sausage meat
- 100 gr or 3.5 oz almond flour
- 50 gr or 1.76 oz celery, finely chopped
- 50 gr or 1.76 oz onions, finely chopped
- 2 cloves garlic, minced (approx. 10 gr or 0.35 oz)
- 1 egg, beaten
- Salt and pepper to taste
- Fresh herbs (rosemary, thyme), chopped

Instructions:

Step 1: Preheat oven to 350°F (175°C).

Step 2: Prepare stuffing by mixing sausage meat, almond flour, celery, onions, garlic, egg, herbs, salt, and pepper.

Step 3: Stuff the capon with the mixture and truss. Place in a roasting pan.

Step 4: Roast for about 2 hours or until the juices run clear.

Step 5: Let rest before carving. Serve with a side of roasted keto-friendly vegetables.

4.Keto Rack of Lamb with Mint Pesto

Yields: 4 servings

Time: 45 minutes

Ingredients:

- 1 rack of lamb (8 ribs, approx. 900 gr or 32 oz)
- 30 ml or 1 oz olive oil
- Salt and freshly ground black pepper to taste

For the Mint Pesto:

- 100 gr or 3.5 oz fresh mint leaves
- 30 gr or 1 oz fresh parsley leaves
- 50 gr or 1.76 oz almonds, blanched
- 2 cloves garlic (approx. 10 gr or 0.35 oz)
- 60 ml or 2 oz extra virgin olive oil
- 30 gr or 1 oz Parmesan cheese, grated

Instructions:

Step 1: Preheat your oven to 400°F (200°C).

Step 2: Season the rack of lamb generously with salt and pepper. Heat olive oil in a large ovenproof skillet over high heat. Sear the lamb on all sides until golden brown, about 2-3 minutes per side.

Step 3: Transfer the skillet to the oven and roast the lamb for about 15-20 minutes for medium-rare or until it reaches the desired doneness.

Step 4: While the lamb is roasting, make the mint pesto. Combine mint leaves, parsley leaves, almonds, and garlic in a food processor. Pulse until coarsely chopped. While the processor is running, gradually add olive oil until the mixture is well blended but still has some texture. Stir in grated Parmesan and season with salt and pepper.

Step 5: Remove the lamb from the oven and let it rest for 10 minutes.

Step 6: Carve the rack into individual ribs and serve with a generous spoonful of mint pesto over each piece.

5. Keto Crab Stuffed Mushrooms with Herb Crust

Yields: 6 servings

Time: 35 minutes

Calories per serving: 220 Kcal

Ingredients:

- 24 large mushrooms (approx. 600 gr or 21 oz total), stems removed

- 200 gr or 7 oz crabmeat, drained and flaked

- 100 gr or 3.5 oz cream cheese, softened

- 50 gr or 1.76 oz Parmesan cheese, grated

- 30 gr or 1 oz almond flour

- 20 gr or 0.7 oz green onions, finely chopped

- 2 cloves garlic, minced (approx. 10 gr or 0.35 oz)

- 30 ml or 1 oz olive oil

- 5 gr or 0.18 oz fresh thyme, chopped

- 5 gr or 0.18 oz fresh parsley, chopped

- Salt and pepper to taste

Instructions:

Step 1: Preheat your oven to 375°F (190°C). Arrange mushroom caps on a baking sheet, drizzle with half the olive oil, and season with salt and pepper.

Step 2: In a bowl, combine crabmeat, cream cheese, Parmesan, almond flour, green onions, half of the garlic, and herbs. Season with salt and pepper to taste.

Step 3: Stuff each mushroom cap generously with the crab mixture.

Step 4: Mix the remaining olive oil and garlic in a small bowl and brush over the stuffed mushrooms. Sprinkle with a little more Parmesan if desired.

Step 5: Bake in the preheated oven for 20 minutes or until the mushrooms are tender and the filling is golden and bubbly.

Step 6: Serve hot, garnished with additional chopped parsley.

Chapter 11: Navigating Common Challenges

Overcoming Repetitiveness in Meals

Maintaining a ketogenic diet for seniors can sometimes lead to a feeling of repetitiveness with meal choices, which may diminish enthusiasm and adherence to the diet. This subchapter explores practical strategies to keep meals interesting and varied, ensuring that the dietary routine remains enjoyable and sustainable.

1. Experiment with New Recipes

Trying new recipes is one of the simplest ways to break the monotony. The internet, keto cookbooks, and community forums offer a wealth of recipe ideas that are both keto-friendly and varied in flavor and ingredients.

- **Action Step**: Dedicate one day each week to trying a new recipe. This will add variety and expand your repertoire of dishes that fit your dietary needs.

2. Incorporate International Flavors

Exploring cuisines from different cultures can introduce new flavors and ingredients, making meals more exciting. Many international dishes can be adapted to fit keto guidelines with a few substitutions.

- **Action Step**: Select a different country each month and explore dishes from that cuisine. For instance, make a keto version of Greek moussaka by substituting the potatoes for eggplant, or try a keto Indian curry using coconut milk and low-carb vegetables.

3. Seasonal and Local Ingredients

Utilizing seasonal and locally available ingredients ensures freshness and varies the diet throughout the year. Seasonal vegetables and meats can provide new inspiration for your meals.

- **Action Step**: Visit local farmers' markets to discover what's in season and plan meals around your finds. This can lead to creative and flavorful dishes that prevent dietary fatigue.

4. Theme Nights

Creating theme nights can make meal planning more fun and anticipated. For example, having a "Fish Friday" or "Meatless Monday" can help structure the dietary week and give people something to look forward to.

- **Action Step**: Plan a weekly theme night and prepare meals that align with that theme. This approach keeps the weekly menu structured yet varied.

5. Involve Friends or Family

Sharing meal preparation with friends or family can introduce new ideas and cooking methods. It's a social way to enhance the meal experience and learn from others' culinary approaches.

- **Action Step**: Organize a weekly dinner with friends or family where everyone contributes a keto-friendly dish. This can be a source of inspiration and a way to enjoy social interactions over food.

6. Rotating Meal Plans

Develop a rotating meal plan that cycles through different dishes over a set period. This will help you plan and alternate dishes in your meals.

Clarifying Common Keto Misconceptions

For seniors embracing a ketogenic lifestyle, misconceptions can create confusion and hinder their progress. This subchapter aims to debunk common myths associated with the ketogenic diet, providing clear and accurate information to ensure seniors can maintain their diet confidently and effectively.

1. Misconception: Keto is Mainly High-Protein

Reality: The ketogenic diet is primarily high-fat, moderate-protein, and very low-carb. Many people mistakenly believe it's similar to other low-carb diets emphasizing high protein. Excessive protein can be converted into glucose in keto, potentially taking you out of ketosis. The focus is on healthy fats to provide energy.

- **Action Step**: Monitor your macronutrient ratio to ensure you consume roughly 70-80% fats, 15-20% protein, and 5-10% carbohydrates.

2. Misconception: Keto Causes Nutrient Deficiency

Reality: Critics often claim that the ketogenic diet lacks nutrients because it restricts certain fruits and vegetables. However, you can achieve a nutrient-rich diet by choosing various low-carb vegetables and supplementing as necessary.

- **Action Step**: Include nutrient-dense, low-carb vegetables like spinach, kale, and broccoli, and consider supplements for fiber, vitamins, and minerals as advised by your healthcare provider.

3. Misconception: Keto is Unsustainable Long-Term

Reality: Some believe that the ketogenic diet is only suitable for short-term weight loss due to its restrictive nature. However, many individuals find keto sustainable because of the variety in food choices and the significant health benefits, such as improved blood sugar control, increased mental clarity, and sustained energy levels.

- **Action Step:** To make keto a sustainable lifestyle choice, focus on incorporating various fats from healthy sources like avocados, coconut oil, and fatty fish. Explore new keto recipes regularly to keep your diet exciting and enjoyable.

4. Misconception: All Fats are Good on Keto

Reality: While the ketogenic diet does emphasize fat intake, the type of fat consumed is crucial. Trans fats and certain saturated fats found in processed foods can harm heart health and overall well-being.

- **Action Step:** Choose healthy fats, such as monounsaturated and polyunsaturated fats in nuts, seeds, olive oil, and fatty fish. Avoid or limit fats from processed snacks, fried foods, and baked goods, which typically contain unhealthy fats.

5. Misconception: Keto Leads to High Cholesterol and Heart Problems

Reality: There is a common concern that the increased fat consumption required by the ketogenic diet could raise cholesterol levels and lead to heart disease. However, research shows that keto can improve heart disease risk factors by reducing triglyceride levels and increasing HDL ("good") cholesterol levels.

- **Action Step:** Regularly monitor your cholesterol levels and consult your healthcare provider to adjust your diet. Include plenty of heart-healthy fats, and ensure you balance your intake with fiber-rich, low-carb vegetables.

6. Misconception: You Can Eat Unlimited Calories on Keto and Still Lose Weight

Reality: Despite its high fat content, calorie intake still matters on the ketogenic diet. Overeating, even with keto-friendly foods, can lead to weight gain or stall weight loss.

- **Action Step:** Track your caloric intake using a food diary or an app to maintain a calorie deficit if weight loss is your goal. Consider portion sizes, especially when consuming high-calorie foods like nuts and cheese.

7. Misconception: Keto is Inappropriate for Those With Certain Health Conditions

Reality: While there are specific conditions where ketogenic diet considerations are necessary (such as type 1 diabetes or pancreatic conditions), many people with chronic illnesses find relief from symptoms through a well-managed keto diet.

- **Action Step:** Always consult with a healthcare professional before starting a ketogenic diet, especially if you have pre-existing health conditions. They can help tailor the diet to your needs and monitor potential health changes.

By understanding and addressing these misconceptions, seniors can more effectively navigate the challenges of maintaining a ketogenic lifestyle and enjoy its health and wellness benefits. This approach ensures they are well-informed and supported in their dietary choices.

Ensuring Accurate and Clear Recipe Measurements

When adopting the ketogenic diet, particularly for seniors, the accuracy of recipe measurements is crucial to maintaining the proper macronutrient balance essential for staying in ketosis. This subchapter addresses the importance of precise measurements in cooking and provides strategies to ensure consistency and success in preparing keto meals.

Importance of Precision in Keto Cooking

Keto recipes require specific ratios of fats, proteins, and carbohydrates. Even minor deviations in ingredient measurements can shift these ratios, potentially affecting the metabolic state of ketosis. Consistent meal preparation is vital for seniors, who may have specific dietary needs to manage health conditions like diabetes or high blood pressure.

Tools for Accurate Measurements

1. **Digital Kitchen Scale:** A digital scale is the most accurate way to measure ingredients, especially for items like meat, nuts, and fats, which can vary significantly in size and density. Weighing ingredients ensures you are consuming the right amount of macros and calories.

Action Step: Invest in a reliable digital kitchen scale and measure all ingredients before cooking. This practice ensures precision and repeatability in your recipes.

2. **Measuring Cups and Spoons:** While less precise than a digital scale, measuring cups and spoons are necessary for liquid and smaller dry ingredients.

Action Step: Use measuring cups for liquids like water, oil, and cream and spoons for minor components like spices and baking powder. Always level off dry ingredients with a knife for accuracy.

Converting Measurements

Many keto recipes might use different units of measurement, depending on the source. Understanding how to convert measurements from one system to another (e.g., grams to ounces, milliliters to fluid ounces) is essential.

Action Step: Keep a conversion chart handy in your kitchen, or use digital tools and apps to convert measurements. This will help you adapt recipes from different sources without error.

Recording and Adjusting Recipes

Recording your modifications and their outcomes as you experiment with different recipes can help refine your culinary skills and ensure consistency.

Action Step: Maintain a recipe journal or a digital document where you track changes made to recipes and their effects on taste and ketosis. This record can guide future cooking and adjustments.

Educational Resources and Practice

Understanding the basics of measurement and conversion is crucial for anyone new to cooking or the keto diet.

Action Step: Consider resources like cooking classes, online tutorials, or keto diet workshops focusing on culinary skills, including accurate measuring and ingredient handling.

By focusing on accurate and precise measurements, seniors can better manage their ketogenic diet, ensuring they enjoy delicious, nutritious meals that support their health goals. This approach not only aids in maintaining nutritional ketosis but empowers seniors to take control of their diet confidently and precisely.

Chapter 12: Enhancing Balance and Stability

Importance of Balance Training for Seniors

Balance training is essential for seniors, mainly as it enhances stability, reduces the risk of falls, and improves quality of life. This subchapter explores why incorporating balance training into a senior's routine is vital, especially alongside a dietary regimen like the ketogenic diet.

Understanding Balance and Aging

As individuals age, several changes occur in the body that can impact balance. Muscle strength decreases, reflexes slow down, and coordination may diminish. These changes can increase the risk of falls, which are a leading cause of severe injuries among seniors. Balance training helps mitigate these risks by improving the body's ability to control and maintain its position, whether moving or still.

Benefits of Balance Training

1. **Fall Prevention:** The most significant benefit of balance training is its ability to prevent falls. By improving stability and coordination, seniors can navigate daily activities more safely and confidently.
2. **Increased Muscle Strength and Flexibility:** Balance exercises often involve muscle strengthening and stretches that enhance overall flexibility, vital for joint health and mobility.
3. **Enhanced Joint Stability:** Balance training helps strengthen the muscles around crucial joints, such as the ankles, knees, and hips, leading to improved joint support and decreased risk of injuries.
4. **Improved Proprioception:** Proprioception is the body's ability to sense its position in space, which diminishes with age. Balance exercises help enhance this sense, which is crucial for performing everyday activities safely.
5. **Boosted Cognitive Functions:** Engaging in physical activities that require balance and concentration supports cognitive health by keeping the mind active.

Integrating Balance Training with a Keto Diet

While supporting weight management and overall health, a ketogenic diet should be complemented with physical exercise to maximize the health benefits for seniors. Balance training, in conjunction with a keto diet, can significantly enhance muscular and metabolic health.

- **Synergistic Effects:** Combining a ketogenic diet and balance training can help reduce inflammation and improve energy efficiency in seniors, making balance exercises more accessible and effective.
- **Weight Management:** Effective weight management through a keto diet can decrease the load on weight-bearing joints, enhance balance, and reduce the risk of falls.

Implementing Balance Exercises

Seniors should start with basic exercises that do not require special equipment and can be performed at home, such as:

- **Standing on One Foot:** Hold onto a chair and gradually decrease support as strength and balance improve.
- **Heel-to-Toe Walk:** This exercise mimics a tightrope walk, which enhances straight-line walking skills.
- **Back Leg Raises:** These strengthen the posterior muscles and improve the support around the hips and lower back.

Action Step: Seniors should aim to incorporate balance training into their routine at least three times a week, gradually increasing the complexity and challenge of the exercises as their balance improves.

Safety Measures

- **Supervised Training:** When starting, it's advisable to perform balance exercises under the supervision of a healthcare professional or a trained instructor.
- **Safe Environment:** Ensure the training area is free of hazards that could cause slips or falls, such as loose rugs or wet floors.
- **Use of Assistive Devices:** Utilize aids like stable chairs or handrails until confidence and balance capabilities improve.

In conclusion, balance training is critical to senior health care, especially when combined with a ketogenic diet. It enhances physical capabilities and safety and contributes to a senior's independence and overall quality of life. This holistic approach to wellness is vital for maintaining mobility, strength, and cognitive function well into the later years of life.

Simple Balance Exercises and Their Benefits

This subchapter focuses on specific balance exercises that are simple and beneficial for seniors, especially those following a ketogenic diet. These exercises are designed to improve stability and strength, enhance overall mobility, and reduce the risk of falls.

1. Toe Stands

Exercise: Stand straight and slowly lift onto your toes, raising your heels off the ground. Hold for a few seconds, then slowly lower back down.

Benefits: Strengthens calf muscles and ankles, which are crucial for balance.

Progression: Start holding onto a chair and gradually try to perform the exercise without support.

2. Heel-to-Toe Walk

Exercise: Place the heel of one foot just in front of the toes of the other foot each time you take a step. Your heel and toes should touch or almost touch.

Benefits: Improves balance and coordination by simulating a narrow walkway, which is common in real-world environments.

Progression: Begin by using a wall for support and gradually walk independently.

3. Single-Leg Balance

Exercise: Stand behind a chair and hold onto the back for support. Lift one foot and balance on the other leg. Hold this position for as long as you can, then switch legs.

Benefits: Enhances leg strength and stabilizes core muscles, improving overall balance.

Progression: Start with short lifts and increase the duration as balance improves.

4. Side Leg Raise

Exercise: Stand behind a chair with feet slightly apart. Slowly lift one leg to the side, keep your back straight and your toes facing forward. Hold and then lower the leg back down.

Benefits: Strengthens hips and thighs, which support the pelvis and improve balance.

Progression: Begin using a chair for support and gradually try to perform the lift without assistance.

5. Back Leg Raises

Exercise: Stand behind a chair and slowly lift one leg straight back without bending your knees or pointing your toes. Hold the position, then lower your leg.

Benefits: Increases back strength, essential for good posture and balance.

Progression: Start by lifting your leg a small amount and increase the height as your balance improves.

6. Standing March

Exercise: Stand in place and slowly march, lifting your knees high towards your chest.

Benefits: Improves coordination and strengthens the lower body, contributing to better stability.

Progression: Begin by holding onto a chair, gradually increasing speed, and lifting your knees higher as you gain confidence.

7. Balancing Wand

Exercise: Hold a stick vertically in one hand and balance on one foot. Focus on keeping the stick upright without swaying.

Benefits: Enhances hand-eye coordination and overall body awareness, which are critical for maintaining balance.

Progression: Use a lighter stick or move to balance without any objects as your skills advance.

Summary

These exercises benefit seniors looking to maintain and enhance their balance and stability. By integrating these simple exercises into a routine, seniors on a ketogenic diet can enjoy increased physical strength and a reduced risk of falls, leading to a higher quality of life and greater independence. Each exercise includes a progression to help seniors advance their balance skills safely and effectively.

Incorporating Balance Workouts into Daily Routine

Incorporating balance workouts into seniors' daily routines is crucial for enhancing their stability and overall quality of life. This subchapter provides strategies for seamlessly integrating balance exercises into everyday activities, ensuring that seniors on a ketogenic diet can maintain both their nutritional goals and physical health.

Understanding the Importance of Regular Practice

Regular balance training can significantly reduce the risk of falls, a primary concern for aging adults. Consistent practice helps build and maintain the muscle strength and coordination necessary for good balance while improving cognitive function through focused movements and body awareness.

Strategies for Incorporating Balance Workouts

1. **Integrate with Everyday Activities:**
   - **While Cooking:** Use the kitchen counter for support while waiting for food to cook, performing side leg raises or standing calf raises.
   - **During TV Commercials:** Stand up and practice toe stands or heel-to-toe walks during commercial breaks.
   - **While Brushing Teeth:** Use the bathroom counter for slight support while standing on one leg or performing mini squats.

2. **Set Specific Times for Balance Training:**
   - **Morning Routine:** Incorporate a five-minute balance circuit every morning after waking up. This can include exercises like single-leg stand or side-leg raises.

   - **Afternoon Breaks:** Use the early afternoon for a quick session of more dynamic balance exercises, such as the standing march or balancing wand, which can also help to boost energy levels for the rest of the day.

   - **Evening Wind Down:** Before bedtime, engage in gentle balance activities like yoga poses or tai chi movements to improve relaxation and sleep quality.

3. **Use Technology to Assist:**
   - **Smartphone Apps:** Use apps for senior fitness, including balance exercises, reminders, and tracking progress.

   - **Online Classes:** Participate in virtual balance workout classes specifically tailored for seniors, which can provide guidance and a sense of community.

4. **Create a Dedicated Space:**
   - **Safe Environment:** Set up a specific area in the home that is safe for balance training, free of obstacles, with a sturdy chair or counter for support if needed.

   - **Accessibility:** Ensure all necessary equipment, such as non-slip mats, comfortable footwear, and props like sticks or balls, are easily accessible.

5. **Involve Family or Friends:**
   - **Group Activities:** Incorporate balance exercises into family gatherings or meetups with friends, such as group walks or partnered balance challenges.

   - **Support Network:** Having a buddy for balance workouts can increase motivation and provide a safety net for trying new exercises.

Benefits of Daily Balance Workouts

- **Improved Mobility:** Daily balance training helps maintain and increase mobility, making everyday activities more accessible and safer.

- **Increased Confidence:** Regular practice improves balance skills, reduces fear of falling, and boosts confidence in physical activities.

- **Enhanced Joint Health:** Balance exercises help strengthen the muscles around joints, reducing the load on joints and alleviating pain.

By making balance workouts a regular part of their daily routine, seniors can remain active, independent, and safe in their environments. This proactive approach to balance and stability enhances physical health and contributes significantly to mental well-being and overall life satisfaction.

APPENDICES

Glossary of Keto Terms in Simple Language

This glossary is designed to help seniors understand standard terms related to the ketogenic diet. The definitions are provided in straightforward language to assist with easy comprehension and application of the keto diet principles.

1. Ketosis:

A metabolic state in which your body uses fat, rather than carbohydrates, as its primary energy source. This occurs when carbohydrate intake is significantly reduced.

2. Ketones/Ketone Bodies:

These are compounds produced by the liver from fatty acids during periods of low food intake, carbohydrate-restrictive diets, or intense exercise. Ketones are an alternative energy source for the brain and body when glucose is scarce.

3. Low-Carb:

A diet that restricts carbohydrates, typically including sugars and starches. It is often rich in protein and fats. The ketogenic diet is a type of low-carb diet but with a greater emphasis on fats.

4. High-Fat:

Describes a diet that includes a high amount of fats from food sources such as butter, cream, coconut oil, and fatty meats. The ketogenic diet typically requires a high fat intake to help maintain ketosis.

5. MCT Oil (Medium-Chain Triglyceride Oil):

A supplement made from a type of fat that is digested more easily than most. It can quickly provide energy and is converted into ketones, making it popular among those following a keto diet.

6. Net Carbs:

The total amount of carbohydrates in a food minus the fiber content is indigestible and thus not considered impactful on blood sugar levels. Calculating net carbs helps manage intake to maintain ketosis.

7. Fat Adaptation:

This is a process by which the body becomes more efficient at burning fat for fuel. It occurs after several weeks of sustained ketosis, resulting in improved energy and stability of fuel supply.

8. Intermittent Fasting (IF):

An eating pattern alternating between eating and fasting periods can enhance the effects of ketosis. It is not a diet but rather a schedule of eating times.

9. Macros (Macronutrients):

These include fats, proteins, and carbohydrates, the three essential components of every diet. The macronutrients are managed carefully to maintain ketosis on a ketogenic diet, with specific ratios depending on individual goals and needs.

10. Bulletproof Coffee:

A high-calorie coffee drink used by keto dieters to increase fat intake. It blends black coffee with butter and coconut oil or MCT oil, often consumed in the morning to boost energy levels.

11. Glycemic Index (GI):

A measure of how much specific foods increase blood sugar levels after eating. Foods with a high GI are typically limited to a ketogenic diet to maintain stable blood sugar and ketosis.

12. Insulin Resistance:

A condition in which the body's cells do not respond effectively to insulin, making it challenging to regulate glucose levels in the blood. A ketogenic diet can help improve insulin sensitivity.

13. Exogenous Ketones:

Supplements containing ketones can be taken to raise the body's ketone levels, providing an immediate source of energy and helping to manage or return to ketosis.

14. Clean Keto:

A version of the ketogenic diet that focuses on whole, unprocessed foods. It prioritizes quality fats and proteins while avoiding artificial additives and low-quality fats.

15. Dirty Keto:

A less restrictive form of the ketogenic diet that allows for processed and fast foods as long as they meet the keto-macronutrient ratios. This approach may still promote ketosis but doesn't focus on the overall nutrient quality of the diet.

This glossary aims to demystify the terminology often associated with the ketogenic diet, making it more accessible to seniors exploring this dietary approach for health and wellness.

Measurement Conversion Tables

For seniors following a ketogenic diet, precise ingredient measurement is crucial to maintaining the correct macronutrient ratios. This section provides helpful conversion tables for common measurements used in cooking and baking, ensuring accuracy and ease in recipe preparation.

Volume Conversions

Common Volumes	Milliliters	Fluid Ounces	Cups	Tablespoons	Teaspoons
1 teaspoon	5 ml	0.17 fl oz	-	-	1
1 tablespoon	15 ml	0.5 fl oz	-	1	3
1/4 cup	59 ml	2 fl oz	0.25	4	12
1/3 cup	79 ml	2.7 fl oz	0.33	5 + 1 tsp	16
1/2 cup	118 ml	4 fl oz	0.5	8	24
1 cup	237 ml	8 fl oz	1	16	48
1 pint	473 ml	16 fl oz	2	32	96
1 quart	946 ml	32 fl oz	4	64	192
1 gallon	3785 ml	128 fl oz	16	256	768

Weight Conversions

Ounces	Grams	Pounds
1 oz	28.35 g	0.0625
2 oz	56.7 g	0.125
4 oz	113.4 g	0.25
8 oz	226.8 g	0.5
16 oz	453.6 g	1

Temperature Conversions

Fahrenheit	Celsius
32°F	0°C
212°F	100°C
250°F	120°C
275°F	135°C
300°F	150°C
325°F	160°C
350°F	175°C
375°F	190°C
400°F	205°C
425°F	220°C
450°F	230°C
475°F	245°C

Useful Tips for Measurement

1. **Accuracy Matters:** Always use the appropriate tools for measurement (e.g., kitchen scales for solids and measuring cups for liquids).

2. **Check Calibration:** Regularly ensure your measuring devices are accurate, especially scales, which can lose calibration over time.

3. **Level Measurements:** When using measuring cups for dry ingredients, always level off the excess with a knife for precision.

4. **Temperature Consistency:** Always check oven temperatures with an oven thermometer, as internal oven thermostats can often be inaccurate.

By using these tables and tips, seniors can accurately measure ingredients, ensuring they adhere to their dietary requirements while enjoying delicious, healthy keto meals.

Bonuses

28-day exercise planner

Here's a customized 28-day exercise plan focusing on simple balance exercises suitable for seniors on a ketogenic diet. The plan aims to enhance balance, flexibility, and strength to support overall health and stability. Each exercise will be described with its benefits, and I'll outline how each movement should be performed.

Week 1-4 Overview:
- **Frequency:** Aim for these exercises 3 days per week (e.g., Monday, Wednesday, Friday).
- **Duration:** Start with sessions lasting about 10-15 minutes, gradually increasing as comfort and stamina improve.
- **Intensity:** Begin at a low intensity, focusing on form and balance, and increase the intensity as your ability improves.

Day 1, 8, 15, 22 - Standing March
Exercise: Stand straight with feet hip-width apart. Lift your right knee towards your chest, then lower it, and repeat with your left knee. Alternate knees as if marching on the spot.
Benefits: Enhances leg strength, balance, and coordination.
Image Description: Senior person standing next to a sturdy chair for support, lifting one knee at a time.

Day 2, 9, 16, 23 - Side Leg Raise
Exercise: Stand beside a chair, holding onto it for support. Slowly lift your right leg to the side, keep your back and legs straight, then lower it back down. Repeat on the left side.

Benefits: Strengthens hips and thighs and improves balance.

Image Description: A senior person stands holding a chair, lifts one leg out to the side, and then brings it back to the middle.

Day 3, 10, 17, 24 - Heel-to-Toe Walk

Exercise: Position your heel right in front of your toe of the opposite foot each time you take a step. Walk this way for 10-15 steps.

Benefits: Improves balance, coordination, and concentration.

Image Description: A senior walking along a straight line, placing one foot directly in front of the other.

Day 4, 11, 18, 25 - Back Leg Raises

Exercise: Stand behind a chair and slowly lift your right leg straight back without bending your knees or pointing your toes. Hold the position, then lower your leg. Repeat with the left leg.

Benefits: Strengthens the lower back and buttock muscles.

Image Description: Senior standing and lifting one leg straight back, holding onto a chair for balance.

Day 5, 12, 19, 26 - Balancing Wand

Exercise: Hold a stick in one hand and stand straight. Balance on one leg while focusing on the stick. Switch the stick to the other hand and the other leg.

Benefits: Improves focus and stability.

Image Description: A senior holding a stick for balance while standing on one leg.

Day 6, 13, 20, 27 - Chair Yoga Poses

Exercise: Perform seated yoga poses such as seated mountain pose, seated twists, and leg lifts.

Benefits: Enhances flexibility, core strength, and mental focus.

Image Description: Senior seated in a chair, performing various yoga stretches and poses.

Day 7, 14, 21, 28 - Rest and Reflection

Exercise: Take this day to rest and reflect on your progress. Consider journaling any changes in your balance and overall mobility.

Benefits: Recovery is crucial for progress and helps prevent overtraining.

Image Description: A senior relaxing in a comfortable chair, perhaps writing in a journal.

This exercise plan is designed to progressively improve balance and stability, which are crucial for seniors, especially those on a ketogenic diet, to maintain mobility and independence. Consult with a healthcare provider before starting any new exercise regimen.

120 Day Meal Planner

Day 1:

- **Breakfast:** Ham and Cheese Egg Cups

- **Lunch:** Keto Chicken Salad with Avocado and Bacon

- **Dinner:** Keto Pesto Chicken Casserole

Day 2:

- **Breakfast:** Coconut Almond Porridge

- **Lunch:** Greek bouyiourdi

- **Dinner:** Stuffed Bell Peppers with Ground Beef and Cauliflower Rice

Day 3:

- **Breakfast:** Keto Bulletproof Coffee

- **Lunch:** Keto Turkey Lettuce Wraps

- **Dinner:** Herb-Crusted Salmon with Creamy Dill Sauce

Day 4:

- **Breakfast:** Keto Avocado Smoothie

- **Lunch:** Keto Cauliflower Soup

- **Dinner:** Keto Lamb Chops with Mint Pesto

Day 5:

- **Breakfast:** Keto Cream Cheese Pancakes

- **Lunch:** Keto Zucchini Noodle Salad

- **Dinner:** Keto Vegetable Frittata

Day 6:

- **Breakfast:** Breakfast Deviled Eggs

- **Lunch:** Keto Beef Stir-Fry

- **Dinner:** Keto Chicken Alfredo with Zucchini Noodles

Day 7:

- **Breakfast:** Keto Avocado Bacon Boats

- **Lunch:** Keto Salmon Salad

- **Dinner:** Keto Creamy Mushroom Soup

Day 8:

- **Breakfast:** Almond Flour Pancakes

- **Lunch:** Keto Tuna Salad Stuffed Tomatoes

- **Dinner:** Keto Chicken Caesar Salad

Day 9:

- **Breakfast:** Keto Breakfast Hash

- **Lunch:** Keto Shrimp and Avocado Salad

- **Dinner:** Keto Cobb Salad

Day 10:

- **Breakfast:** Avocado and Egg Salad

- **Lunch:** Keto Salmon Spinach Salad

- **Dinner:** Keto Stuffed Bell Peppers

Day 11:

- **Breakfast:** Chia Pudding with Berries

- **Lunch:** Keto Turkey and Avocado Wraps

- **Dinner:** Keto Cream of Broccoli Soup

Day 12:

- **Breakfast:** Keto Lemon Ricotta Pancakes

- **Lunch:** Keto Lemon Herb Grilled Chicken

- **Dinner:** Keto Smoked Salmon Platter

Day 13:

- **Breakfast:** Keto Porridge

- **Lunch:** Keto Avocado Shrimp Salad

- **Dinner:** Keto Mediterranean Chicken Skillet

Day 14:

- **Breakfast:** Keto Cheese Pancakes

- **Lunch:** Keto Lemon Garlic Shrimp

- **Dinner:** Keto Balsamic Beef Pot Roast

Day 15:

- **Breakfast:** Keto Sausage and Egg Breakfast Skillet

- **Lunch:** Keto Creamy Tuscan Chicken

- **Dinner:** Keto Smoked Salmon Frittata

Day 16:

- **Breakfast:** Keto Ham and Cheese Muffins

- **Lunch:** Keto Garlic Butter Pork Tenderloin

- **Dinner:** Keto Stuffed Capon

Day 17:

- **Breakfast:** Keto Chocolate Mousse

- **Lunch:** Keto Salmon Nicoise Salad

- **Dinner:** Keto Ratatouille with Grilled Chicken

Day 18:

- **Breakfast:** Keto Lemon Bars

- **Lunch:** Keto Stuffed Avocados with Crabmeat

- **Dinner:** Keto Mushroom and Swiss Chard Stuffed Pork Tenderloin

Day 19:

- **Breakfast:** Keto Cheesecake Bites

- **Lunch:** Keto Thai Coconut Shrimp Soup

- **Dinner:** Keto Lemon Butter Seared Scallops

Day 20:

- **Breakfast:** Keto Coconut Clusters

- **Lunch:** Keto Lemon-Herb Roasted Chicken

- **Dinner:** Keto Cauliflower Steak with Chimichurri Sauce

Day 21:

- **Breakfast:** Keto Peanut Butter Cups

- **Lunch:** Keto Bacon-Wrapped Asparagus with Hollandaise

- **Dinner:** Keto Cheese and Herb Stuffed Mushrooms

Day 22:

- **Breakfast:** Keto Almond Joy Bars

- **Lunch:** Keto Bacon-Wrapped Jalapeño Poppers

- **Dinner:** Keto Olive Tapenade with Flaxseed Crackers

Day 23:

- **Breakfast:** Keto Cinnamon Roll Fat Bombs

- **Lunch:** Keto Spiced Nuts

- **Dinner:** Keto Avocado Chips

Day 34:

- **Breakfast:** Keto Raspberry Gelatin Dessert

- **Lunch:** Keto Chocolate Avocado Truffles

- **Dinner:** Keto Mini Blueberry Cheesecakes

Day 35:

- **Breakfast:** Keto Avocado Bacon Boats

- **Lunch:** Keto Chicken Caesar Salad

- **Dinner:** Keto Pesto Chicken Casserole

Day 36:

- **Breakfast:** Coconut Almond Porridge

- **Lunch:** Keto Turkey and Avocado Wraps

- **Dinner:** Keto Lamb Chops with Mint Pesto

Day 37:

- **Breakfast:** Keto Bulletproof Coffee

- **Lunch:** Greek bouyiourdi

- **Dinner:** Stuffed Bell Peppers with Ground Beef and Cauliflower Rice

Day 38:

- **Breakfast:** Keto Cream Cheese Pancakes

- **Lunch:** Keto Salmon Salad

- **Dinner:** Herb-Crusted Salmon with Creamy Dill Sauce

Day 39:

- **Breakfast:** Breakfast Deviled Eggs

- **Lunch:** Keto Zucchini Noodle Salad

- **Dinner:** Keto Chicken Alfredo with Zucchini Noodles

Day 40:

- **Breakfast:** Keto Porridge

- **Lunch:** Keto Beef Stir-Fry

- **Dinner:** Keto Vegetable Frittata

Day 41:

- **Breakfast:** Almond Flour Pancakes

- **Lunch:** Keto Cauliflower Soup

- **Dinner:** Keto Creamy Mushroom Soup

Day 42:

- **Breakfast:** Keto Lemon Ricotta Pancakes

- **Lunch:** Keto Tuna Salad Stuffed Tomatoes

- **Dinner:** Keto Cobb Salad

Day 44:

- **Breakfast:** Keto Sausage and Egg Breakfast Skillet

- **Lunch:** Keto Shrimp and Avocado Salad

- **Dinner:** Keto Stuffed Bell Peppers

Day 45:

- **Breakfast:** Keto Cheese Pancakes

- **Lunch:** Keto Lemon Herb Grilled Chicken

- **Dinner:** Keto Smoked Salmon Platter

Day 46:

- **Breakfast:** Keto Ham and Cheese Muffins

- **Lunch:** Keto Garlic Butter Pork Tenderloin

- **Dinner:** Keto Stuffed Capon

Day 47:

- **Breakfast:** Keto Peanut Butter Smoothie

- **Lunch:** Keto Rack of Lamb with Mint Pesto

- **Dinner:** Keto Crab Stuffed Mushrooms with Herb Crust

Day 48:

- **Breakfast:** Keto Lemon Poppyseed Muffins

- **Lunch:** Keto Beef Wellington

- **Dinner:** Keto Garlic and Herb Grilled Lamb Chops

Day 49:

- **Breakfast:** Keto Chocolate Pancakes

- **Lunch:** Keto Stuffed Capon

- **Dinner:** Keto Duck Breast with Red Wine Reduction

Day 50:

- **Breakfast:** Keto Cinnamon Roll Pancakes

- **Lunch:** Keto Coconut Curry Chicken

- **Dinner:** Keto Walnut-Crusted Pork Tenderloin

Day 51:

- **Breakfast:** Keto Vanilla Chia Pudding

- **Lunch:** Keto Lemon Herb Roasted Chicken

- **Dinner:** Keto Spicy Beef Stir-Fry

Day 52:

- **Breakfast:** Keto Blueberry Muffins

- **Lunch:** Keto Smoked Salmon and Avocado Towers

- **Dinner:** Keto Parmesan-Crusted Halibut

Day 53:

- **Breakfast:** Keto Chocolate Mousse

- **Lunch:** Keto Salmon Nicoise Salad

- **Dinner:** Keto Ratatouille with Grilled Chicken

Day 54:

- **Breakfast:** Keto Lemon Bars

- **Lunch:** Keto Stuffed Avocados with Crabmeat

- **Dinner:** Keto Mushroom and Swiss Chard Stuffed Pork Tenderloin

Day 55:

- **Breakfast:** Keto Cheesecake Bites

- **Lunch:** Keto Thai Coconut Shrimp Soup

- **Dinner:** Keto Lemon Butter Seared Scallops

Day 56:

- **Breakfast:** Keto Coconut Clusters

- **Lunch:** Keto Lemon-Herb Roasted Chicken

- **Dinner:** Keto Cauliflower Steak with Chimichurri Sauce

Day 57:

- **Breakfast:** Keto Peanut Butter Cups

- **Lunch:** Keto Bacon-Wrapped Asparagus with Hollandaise

- **Dinner:** Keto Cheese and Herb Stuffed Mushrooms

Day 58:

- **Breakfast:** Keto Ham and Cheese Muffins

- **Lunch:** Keto Zucchini Noodle Salad

- **Dinner:** Keto Lemon Herb Roasted Chicken

Day 59:

- **Breakfast:** Keto Porridge

- **Lunch:** Keto Cobb Salad

- **Dinner:** Keto Beef Wellington

Day 60:

- **Breakfast:** Keto Bulletproof Coffee

- **Lunch:** Keto Thai Coconut Shrimp Soup

- **Dinner:** Keto Stuffed Capon

Day 61:

- **Breakfast:** Keto Blueberry Muffins

- **Lunch:** Keto Lemon Butter Seared Scallops

- **Dinner:** Keto Balsamic Beef Pot Roast

Day 62:

- **Breakfast:** Keto Lemon Ricotta Pancakes

- **Lunch:** Keto Rack of Lamb with Mint Pesto

- **Dinner:** Keto Creamy Mushroom Soup

Day 63:

- **Breakfast:** Keto Peanut Butter Smoothie

- **Lunch:** Keto Chicken Caesar Salad

- **Dinner:** Keto Smoked Salmon Platter

Day 64:

- **Breakfast:** Keto Avocado Smoothie

- **Lunch:** Keto Turkey Lettuce Wraps

- **Dinner:** Stuffed Bell Peppers with Ground Beef and Cauliflower Rice

Day 65:

- **Breakfast:** Keto Chocolate Mousse

- **Lunch:** Keto Salmon Nicoise Salad

- **Dinner:** Keto Chicken Alfredo with Zucchini Noodles

Day 66:

- **Breakfast:** Keto Almond Joy Bars

- **Lunch:** Keto Beef Stir-Fry

- **Dinner:** Keto Vegetable Frittata

Day 67:

- **Breakfast:** Keto Avocado Bacon Boats

- **Lunch:** Greek bouyiourdi

- **Dinner:** Herb-Crusted Salmon with Creamy Dill Sauce

Day 68:

- **Breakfast:** Keto Lemon Poppyseed Muffins

- **Lunch:** Keto Tuna Salad Stuffed Tomatoes

- **Dinner:** Keto Lamb Chops with Mint Pesto

Day 69:

- **Breakfast:** Keto Cheese Pancakes

- **Lunch:** Keto Shrimp and Avocado Salad

- **Dinner:** Keto Pesto Chicken Casserole

Day 70:

- **Breakfast:** Keto Sausage and Egg Breakfast Skillet

- **Lunch:** Keto Cauliflower Soup

- **Dinner:** Keto Garlic and Herb Grilled Lamb Chops

Day 71:

- **Breakfast:** Keto Cinnamon Roll Pancakes

- **Lunch:** Keto Lemon Herb Grilled Chicken

- **Dinner:** Keto Walnut-Crusted Pork Tenderloin

Day 72:

- **Breakfast:** Keto Chocolate Pancakes

- **Lunch:** Keto Coconut Curry Chicken

- **Dinner:** Keto Duck Breast with Red Wine Reduction

Day 73:

- **Breakfast:** Keto Vanilla Chia Pudding

- **Lunch:** Keto Smoked Salmon and Avocado Towers

- **Dinner:** Keto Parmesan-Crusted Halibut

Day 74:

- **Breakfast:** Keto Raspberry Gelatin Dessert

- **Lunch:** Keto Ratatouille with Grilled Chicken

- **Dinner:** Keto Mushroom and Swiss Chard Stuffed Pork Tenderloin

Day 75:

- **Breakfast:** Keto Cheesecake Bites

- **Lunch:** Keto Stuffed Avocados with Crabmeat

- **Dinner:** Keto Stuffed Bell Peppers

Day 76:

- **Breakfast:** Keto Coconut Clusters

- **Lunch:** Keto Chicken Alfredo with Zucchini Noodles

- **Dinner:** Keto Lemon Herb Roasted Chicken

Day 77:

- **Breakfast:** Keto Peanut Butter Cups

- **Lunch:** Keto Beef Stir-Fry

- **Dinner:** Keto Smoked Salmon Platter

Day 78:

- **Breakfast:** Keto Almond Joy Bars

- **Lunch:** Greek bouyiourdi

- **Dinner:** Keto Pesto Chicken Casserole

Day 79:

- **Breakfast:** Keto Avocado Smoothie

- **Lunch:** Keto Turkey Lettuce Wraps

- **Dinner:** Stuffed Bell Peppers with Ground Beef and Cauliflower Rice

Day 80:

- **Breakfast:** Keto Blueberry Muffins

- **Lunch:** Keto Cobb Salad

- **Dinner:** Keto Balsamic Beef Pot Roast

Day 81:

- **Breakfast:** Keto Lemon Ricotta Pancakes

- **Lunch:** Keto Rack of Lamb with Mint Pesto

- **Dinner:** Keto Creamy Mushroom Soup

Day 82:

- **Breakfast:** Keto Porridge

- **Lunch:** Keto Chicken Caesar Salad

- **Dinner:** Keto Smoked Salmon Platter

Day 83:

- **Breakfast:** Keto Bulletproof Coffee

- **Lunch:** Keto Thai Coconut Shrimp Soup

- **Dinner:** Keto Stuffed Capon

Day 84:

- **Breakfast:** Keto Peanut Butter Smoothie

- **Lunch:** Keto Lemon Butter Seared Scallops

- **Dinner:** Keto Lamb Chops with Mint Pesto

Day 85:

- **Breakfast:** Keto Lemon Poppyseed Muffins

- **Lunch:** Keto Tuna Salad Stuffed Tomatoes

- **Dinner:** Keto Pesto Chicken Casserole

Day 86:

- **Breakfast:** Keto Cream Cheese Pancakes

- **Lunch:** Keto Lemon Herb Grilled Chicken

- **Dinner:** Keto Beef Stir-Fry

Day 87:

- **Breakfast:** Keto Bulletproof Coffee

- **Lunch:** Keto Zucchini Noodle Salad

- **Dinner:** Keto Smoked Salmon Platter

Day 88:

- **Breakfast:** Keto Blueberry Muffins

- **Lunch:** Greek bouyiourdi

- **Dinner:** Herb-Crusted Salmon with Creamy Dill Sauce

Day 89:

- **Breakfast:** Keto Lemon Ricotta Pancakes

- **Lunch:** Keto Turkey Lettuce Wraps

- **Dinner:** Keto Pesto Chicken Casserole

Day 90:

- **Breakfast:** Keto Avocado Smoothie

- **Lunch:** Keto Chicken Caesar Salad

- **Dinner:** Stuffed Bell Peppers with Ground Beef and Cauliflower Rice

Day 91:

- **Breakfast:** Keto Chocolate Mousse

- **Lunch:** Keto Cobb Salad

- **Dinner:** Keto Creamy Mushroom Soup

Day 92:

- **Breakfast:** Keto Almond Joy Bars

- **Lunch:** Keto Thai Coconut Shrimp Soup

- **Dinner:** Keto Lamb Chops with Mint Pesto

Day 93:

- **Breakfast:** Keto Peanut Butter Smoothie

- **Lunch:** Keto Stuffed Avocados with Crabmeat

- **Dinner:** Keto Balsamic Beef Pot Roast

Day 94:

- **Breakfast:** Keto Lemon Poppyseed Muffins

- **Lunch:** Keto Rack of Lamb with Mint Pesto

- **Dinner:** Keto Vegetable Frittata

Day 95:

- **Breakfast:** Keto Cheese Pancakes

- **Lunch:** Keto Stuffed Capon

- **Dinner:** Keto Walnut-Crusted Pork Tenderloin

Day 96:

- **Breakfast:** Keto Sausage and Egg Breakfast Skillet

- **Lunch:** Keto Salmon Nicoise Salad

- **Dinner:** Keto Garlic and Herb Grilled Lamb Chops

Day 97:

- **Breakfast:** Keto Cinnamon Roll Pancakes

- **Lunch:** Keto Beef Wellington

- **Dinner:** Keto Duck Breast with Red Wine Reduction

Day 98:

- **Breakfast:** Keto Chocolate Pancakes

- **Lunch:** Keto Coconut Curry Chicken

- **Dinner:** Keto Parmesan-Crusted Halibut

Day 99:

- **Breakfast:** Keto Vanilla Chia Pudding

- **Lunch:** Keto Smoked Salmon and Avocado Towers

- **Dinner:** Keto Ratatouille with Grilled Chicken

Day 100:

- **Breakfast:** Keto Raspberry Gelatin Dessert

- **Lunch:** Keto Mushroom and Swiss Chard Stuffed Pork Tenderloin

- **Dinner:** Keto Stuffed Bell Peppers

Day 101:

- **Breakfast:** Keto Cheesecake Bites

- **Lunch:** Keto Chicken Alfredo with Zucchini Noodles

- **Dinner:** Keto Lemon Herb Roasted Chicken

Day 102:

- **Breakfast:** Keto Coconut Clusters

- **Lunch:** Keto Beef Stir-Fry

- **Dinner:** Keto Smoked Salmon Platter

Day 103:

- **Breakfast:** Keto Peanut Butter Cups

- **Lunch:** Greek bouyiourdi

- **Dinner:** Keto Pesto Chicken Casserole

Day 104:

- **Breakfast:** Keto Almond Joy Bars

- **Lunch:** Keto Turkey Lettuce Wraps

- **Dinner:** Stuffed Bell Peppers with Ground Beef and Cauliflower Rice

Day 105:

- **Breakfast:** Keto Avocado Smoothie

- **Lunch:** Keto Chicken Caesar Salad

- **Dinner:** Keto Balsamic Beef Pot Roast

Day 106:

- **Breakfast:** Keto Blueberry Muffins

- **Lunch:** Keto Cobb Salad

- **Dinner:** Keto Creamy Mushroom Soup

Day 107:

- **Breakfast:** Keto Lemon Ricotta Pancakes

- **Lunch:** Keto Thai Coconut Shrimp Soup

- **Dinner:** Keto Lamb Chops with Mint Pesto

Day 108:

- **Breakfast:** Keto Bulletproof Coffee

- **Lunch:** Keto Stuffed Avocados with Crabmeat

- **Dinner:** Keto Walnut-Crusted Pork Tenderloin

Day 109:

- **Breakfast:** Keto Lemon Poppyseed Muffins

- **Lunch:** Keto Rack of Lamb with Mint Pesto

- **Dinner:** Keto Vegetable Frittata

Day 110:

- **Breakfast:** Keto Cheese Pancakes

- **Lunch:** Keto Stuffed Capon

- **Dinner:** Keto Garlic and Herb Grilled Lamb Chops

Day 111:

- **Breakfast:** Keto Sausage and Egg Breakfast Skillet

- **Lunch:** Keto Beef Wellington

- **Dinner:** Keto Duck Breast with Red Wine Reduction

Day 112:

- **Breakfast:** Keto Cinnamon Roll Pancakes

- **Lunch:** Keto Coconut Curry Chicken

- **Dinner:** Keto Parmesan-Crusted Halibut

Day 113:

- **Breakfast:** Keto Cream Cheese Pancakes

- **Lunch:** Keto Chicken Caesar Salad

- **Dinner:** Keto Lamb Chops with Mint Pesto

Day 114:

- **Breakfast:** Keto Blueberry Muffins

- **Lunch:** Keto Smoked Salmon and Avocado Towers

- **Dinner:** Keto Vegetable Frittata

Day 115:

- **Breakfast:** Keto Chocolate Mousse

- **Lunch:** Keto Zucchini Noodle Salad

- **Dinner:** Keto Garlic and Herb Grilled Lamb Chops

Day 116:

- **Breakfast:** Keto Almond Joy Bars

- **Lunch:** Greek bouyiourdi

- **Dinner:** Keto Balsamic Beef Pot Roast

Day 117:

- **Breakfast:** Keto Peanut Butter Smoothie

- **Lunch:** Keto Beef Stir-Fry

- **Dinner:** Stuffed Bell Peppers with Ground Beef

Day 118:

- **Breakfast:** Keto Bulletproof Coffee

- **Lunch:** Keto Turkey Lettuce Wraps

- **Dinner:** Herb-Crusted Salmon with Creamy Dill Sauce

Day 119:

- **Breakfast:** Keto Cinnamon Roll Pancakes

- **Lunch:** Keto Lemon Herb Grilled Chicken

- **Dinner:** Keto Creamy Tuscan Chicken

Day 120:

- **Breakfast:** Keto Vanilla Chia Pudding

- **Lunch:** Keto Rack of Lamb with Mint Pesto

- **Dinner:** Keto Smoked Salmon Frittata

Copyright Disclaimer

Made in United States
Troutdale, OR
08/25/2024